Sir Edward Burr

Saint Frides
Window

Christ Church Cathedral, Oxford

Ruth Buckley

Sir Edward Burne-Jones
St Frideswide Window
Christ Church Cathedral, Oxford

Published by
Palmcross Publications
www.palmcrosspublications.co.uk
e-mail palmcross@aol.co.uk

Front Cover
Column 2, panel 1 of St Frideswide window © John Buckley
Back cover
Column 3, panel 1 of St Frideswide window © John Buckley

Printed by
MP Printers, Thame, Oxfordshire, UK
www.mp-printers.co.uk

For further information on St Frideswide
www.frideswide.org.uk

Contents

Acknowledgements

Illustrations

All photographs © 2021 John and Ruth Buckley, unless otherwise stated.

P 33. Etching of Oseney Abbey, Oxford County Council photographic archive. By kind permission. HT 13582.

P 35. John Ruskin 1863, copyright holder unknown.

P 37. Burne Jones window, St Columba's Topcliffe. By kind permission of the churchwarden.

P 38. Good Shepherd cartoon, © Victoria and Albert Museum, London. By kind permission.
Good shepherd panel photo © John Buckley. Courtesy Birmingham Museums Trust

P 40. Cartoon Jones / Morris: Topsy and Ned, settled on the settle in Red Lion Square, by Max Beerbohm from Rossetti and his Circle by Max Beerbohm.

P 41. Etching of Latin chapel from Oxford Cathedral and See, by Percy Dearmer 1899.

P 54. First Cartoon of Frideswide window, © Aberdeen Art Gallery. By kind permission.

P60. Frideswide Cartoon Screen. Photograph donated to Cheltenham Ladies' College by the owner Sarah Glasson. Permission of owner was sought but could not be obtained because of the death of Sarah Glasson.

P 64. W Graham Robertson, frontispiece from his autobiography Time Was, 1931.

Thanks

Christ Church Cathedral: Thanks are given to the Dean and Chapter, Vergers, and Archivist for their encouragement and inspiration and allowing access to, and photography of, the Frideswide window.

Cheltenham Ladies' College: Thanks are given to the Principal and Archivist who allowed access to the Council Meeting Chamber, and photography of, the St Frideswide window cartoons, as well as providing information about the provenance of the work.

Bradfield College: Thanks are given to the Headmaster and Archivist for access to and information about the Burne Jones window in the dining hall and for allowing photography of the window.

Foreword

When St Augustine put his foot on the seashore in Kent in 597AD he brought with him a new religious movement that spread across the whole of England. But, with a mostly illiterate population, the monks sent over from Rome had to find a way to spread the faith by word of mouth alone. Their first resort was to the precious, hand-written gospel books they brought with them. Full of stories that were easy to tell and easy to pass on, theirs was an oral tradition of faith. It was not long before these Dark Age pioneers were made saints themselves and stories of St Cuthbert, St Aiden and St Hilda, to name just a few, were told and retold. These were stories of faith, prayer and resistance to temptation. Stories of endurance and even of healings.

Oxford is fortunate enough to have a saint of its own. Her name in Old English was Frithes-Wytha. It gradually changed to Frides-Wida and then Frideswide, as she is known today. This is an authentic Anglo-Saxon name which has been linked with the site of her monastery in Oxford since the eighth century. However, although Frideswide was eventually made the Patron Saint of Oxford and of the University in 1434, and the Pope recognised her cult in 1480, the connection between Oxford and its saint has had a very chequered history.

Her cult, which started in her lifetime, was based around miracles of healing, and probably continued into the ninth century. The Viking incursions destroyed many monastic communities and, although St Frideswide's was initially spared, her monastery languished through the tenth century and eventually suffered an apocalyptic fire in the early eleventh century. It was revived by the foundation of the Augustinian Priory of Saint Frideswide in 1122, the building of a magnificent new church on the site of her original church in 1170-1200, and the construction of a wonderful, decorated shrine, dedicated on 12th February 1180, where healing miracles occurred.

We are fortunate indeed to still have the twelfth century Priory Church of St Frideswide, which survived the dissolution of the monasteries when it was transformed by King Henry VIII into the cathedral of the new diocese of Oxford in 1546. But, as with many early English saints, the shrine was destroyed in 1538 and, for the next 300 years, Oxford's Patron Saint slid into obscurity. From earliest times, stories of the saints were portrayed in art and immortalised through magnificent buildings and St Frideswide's was no exception. Images and carvings that depicted her did survive inside the church, but it took a glowing, mid-nineteenth century, stained-glass window and the reconstruction of her shrine to bring Saint Frideswide back from the shadows, to tell her story once again.

Now, with the uncertainties of life in the twenty-first century, we are rediscovering and reconnecting with the certainties of the past, and Oxford's first known resident is an important symbol of perseverance and leadership through her dedication and commitment to a cause. Her life of selfless devotion to God and to others continues to be remembered in the cathedral with a Patronal Festival every year on or near the 19th of October, her Saint's Day.

Ruth Buckley

A Legendary Princess

Frideswide was an Anglo-Saxon princess, the daughter of a sub-king of Mercia. It is believed that his territory was in the Upper Thames valley and included the junction of the Thames and Cherwell. The earliest records indicate that he was a convert to the new religion of Christianity and built a small monastery to show his devotion to his faith. His daughter, the princess Frideswide, became the first abbess. This was in the late seventh or early eighth centuries, but the only date recorded in the historic documents is 727AD. Unfortunately, of the two legends that record the date 727, one mentions it as her birth and the other as her death, so we are none the wiser. The most prolific time of monastery building was between 680AD and 735AD, and her lifespan was almost certainly within that timeframe.

At this time the pre-Oxford location was in the Anglo-Saxon kingdom of Mercia which converted to Christianity in 653AD. The Kings Wulfhere (658-675), Æthelred (675-704) and Ethelbald (716-757) were the most prominent Christian Mercian kings. This local sub-king is very likely to have had connections with the royal family of Mercians and the dates of his service may fit with the reign of Æthelred, while Frideswide was living during the reign of Ethelbald. All these kings endowed monasteries and granted land to their generals (sub-kings) to do the same.

Frideswide's father's true name is unknown, but he was given the name of Dydan (or Didan) when her legend was recorded in the twelfth century. Unfortunately, the site of his palace has been lost. Royal Anglo-Saxon sites have been located at Benson and Sutton Courtenay, but these were in the region the West Saxons, the rivals of the Mercians. Historians have favoured Eynsham or Bampton, but the closest place of antiquity north of the Thames is Headington, which has a history of settlement going back to Roman times. However, Anglo-Saxon remains, and a 6th century burial have been found there. It is a good choice for the headquarters of a South Mercian king, being on higher ground close to a Roman Road between Alchester (near Bicester) and Dorchester, yet near to his southern border, the Thames. It was also a more defensible site than on the river plain, and closer to an important crossing of the Thames than Eynsham or Bampton.

The Anglo-Saxon name of Frithes-Wytha is a conjunction of Frithes, meaning Peace, and Wytha, Wida or With, meaning a strong connection or agreement. There were continual battles at this period of history and Dydan is likely to have been frequently at war with the Saxons south of the Thames. For his daughter to be named Peace Strong, Peace Connection or Peace Agreement sounds as though he was torn between his duty to fight and his new Christian faith which advocated peace.

The site Oxford now inhabits was an almost impassable flood plain in the seventh century, with wide marshy areas on either side of the river Thames. However, a peninsula of raised, dry gravel running north-to-south between the Thames and Cherwell rivers was an ideal spot for a secluded religious house. Although access to it was restricted and only from the north, it was in a prominent position, and may have been a sacred landscape as a large henge was found just to the north (under St John's college) dating to around 2,300BC. Evidence for occupation of the same period has also been found under the Old Radcliffe Infirmary and University Parks nearby, and Anglo-Saxon occupation has also been identified.[1] Archaeology has shown the flood plain to have been around twenty feet lower in the Saxon period than today. The site also rises, and the high altar of the cathedral is around twelve feet above Broad Walk, giving any early building placed there a commanding view, over thirty feet altogether, above the meadows to the south.

The early monastery appears to have consisted of a church with living accommodation, supported by the grant of lands and property from the king. It now lies beneath the site of Christ Church Cathedral, and no trace of it has been identified. It would have been a short ride by horse downhill from Headington, and Dydan could have easily overseen his building-work and later visited his daughter Frideswide, when she became abbess. The commanding position of the church and its surrounding buildings was also a sign to travellers that they were entering Mercian territory.

In many ways it was an ideal location, perfect for a monastic life of prayer and devotion to God, being protected on the south, east and west by the marshy river plain. A crossing of the Thames soon developed to the south (the present-day Folly Bridge), and the west (Hythe Bridge, close to the original Oxenford). These crossings were used by the many early pilgrims attracted by the miracles associated with St Frideswide and became more permanent and substantial with the growth of the early city.

The royal lords of the Anglo-Saxon period frequently put their female relatives in charge of their new foundations. They and their men were continually at war, and these women were the most appropriate leaders to maintain the economic, social, and religious integrity and prosperity of their lord's property while they were away. These high ranking and pious ladies became influential in their own right, and many were later canonised as saints. Frideswide, who according to the legend was taught to be a devout Christian in childhood, was the perfect candidate for the position of abbess in this important border region.

There were other examples of newly established religious houses at Bicester, Thame, and Abingdon to inspire her. Bicester and Aylesbury were run by abbesses who were relatives of King Wulfhere and his brother King Æthelred and, who knows, they might have been distant relatives of Frideswide herself. Many early monasteries run by these royal abbesses were double houses of monks and nuns, but legend records that Frideswide invited twelve of her female friends to become nuns with her, so it was actually a nunnery at its inception. At this early stage there were no monastic orders as such, but she is thought to have run her establishment with a rule of seclusion, chastity, prayer and devotion to God.

Frideswide, despite her decision to leave the world, was still a royal princess and an only child and would inherit her father's wealth. She was potentially an important marriage partner for a subsequent king and her legend describes how she fled from an importunate lover (later called King Algar), who wished to marry her and would not take 'No' for an answer. Some versions of her legend suggest he applied to her father, King Dydan for her hand, some say that he was a new king who had taken over at Dydan's death. I prefer the latter version, as Algar's conquest of her would have secured him wealth and land as well as the loyalty of her followers and would have underlined his authority as the new ruler. It explains his incandescent anger at being refused. It is also unlikely that King Dydan, if he was still alive, would have allowed his daughter to be driven out of the monastery he had built for her, and chased around the countryside by a young upstart wanting to marry her. No, if she were to be married, her father would have arranged it.

But Frideswide had, in effect, been married to God when she became an abbess and there was no way she was going to give up her calling. Her desperate prayers to God for rescue at the point of capture, resulted in a miracle when King Algar was struck blind. The various versions of her legend differ over whether he repented of his wrong-doing or remained blind all his life, but he stopped pursuing Frideswide, and she returned to her nunnery.

This was a seriously significant miracle which occurred at the North Gate, a major entry point. This was probably the main gate of the monastery, rather than the town, as the settlement was small and probably stood outside the nunnery enclosure. It was observed by many members of the local population and was so profound that legend records that future kings of England, up to the 12th century at least, refused to enter Oxford for fear of blindness. Undeterred, her life of prayer was accompanied by further healing miracles, and her fame spread. As an early following of pilgrims crowded into the small urban area surrounding the nunnery, it stimulated economic growth. The city was first named Oxenford, because of the Thames crossing, and grew into the Oxford we know today.

As the first person known to have lived on the historic site of Oxford, Frideswide is now looked upon as the founder of the city, but the thirteen hundred years since her death has seen enormous variations in her importance in the history of the city and in the attention paid to her. Despite the fact that Oxford owes its location and existence to her, and the Priory Church of Saint Frideswide (now Christ Church Cathedral) was built in her honour and stands as a huge memorial to her faith, her memory was shunned for hundreds of years. Although Frideswide has been the official Patron Saint of Oxford City and Oxford University since 1434, and the Pope recognised her cult in 1480, the dissolution of the monasteries, barely sixty years later between 1536 and 1541, resulted in the destruction of her relics and shrine in 1538 and suppressed her memory. For over three hundred years there was little to remind people she had ever existed.

It took a legacy from John Bull, a Canon of Christ Church in the mid-19th century, and the skill of an unknown artist, to bring the legend of Saint Frideswide back to life with the construction of the Frideswide window. The choice of the artist/designer is an interesting one because, although his potential can be seen in the window, the Cathedral was taking a gamble on plain Ned Jones, the protégé of the flamboyant artist Dante Gabriel Rossetti, an influential founding member of the art movement called the Pre-Raphaelites.

The Frideswide window was one of the first stained-glass windows that Ned Jones designed, and there is much to criticise about it when viewed with 21st century eyes. Later, at the height of his career, his sublime figures of saints and angels, literary figures and mythical heroes were incomparable. They adorn four further windows in Oxford cathedral and many more in colleges and chapels across Oxford, and across the whole of England. However, this window was only the fourth he had ever designed and is quite different from later examples of his art and is worthy of study for that reason alone.

Edward Burne Jones did not have a hyphen in his name until February 1894 when he legally hyphenated it prior to accepting a knighthood on 3rd May 1894. He is therefore referred to without the hyphen in the majority of this book, as that was his name at the time of the design and construction of the window. But, as an early work of the toweringly famous Sir Edward Coley Burne-Jones, the Frideswide window is a wonderful treasure and deserves to be properly understood.

The Window

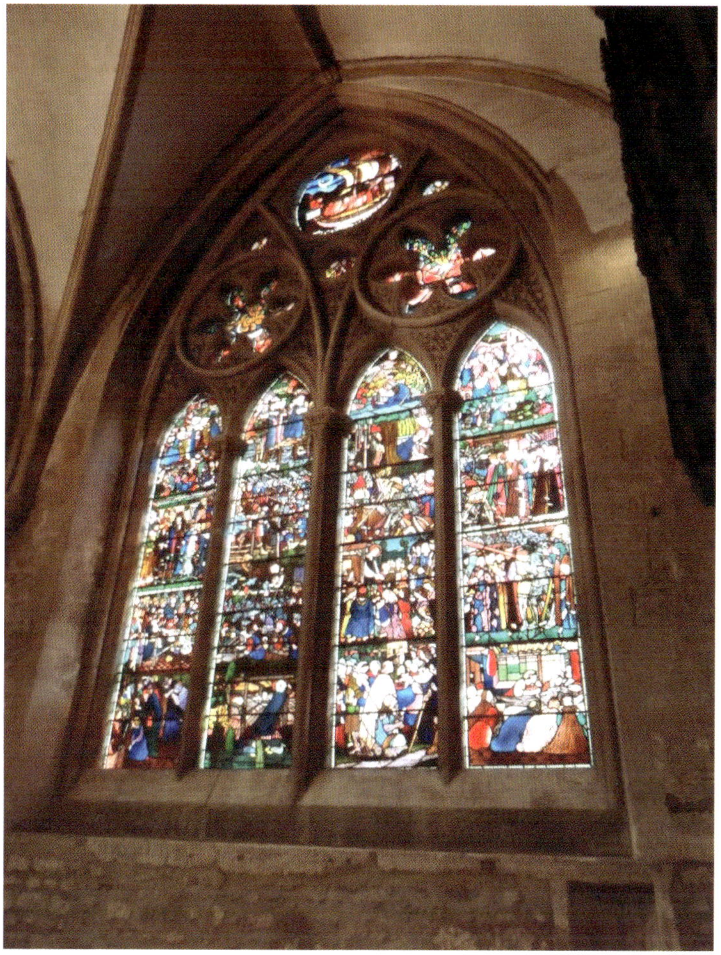

The Frideswide window is a large, brightly coloured stained-glass window with four vertical columns, surmounted by elegant tracery. It has a large roundel in the top position, two six-petalled lights, one on either side, and three small roundels spaced between them.

At first sight, and from a distance the four vertical lights appear full of a mosaic of coloured shapes with little meaning, but after looking at it for a few moments, figures begin to stand out. There are four panels in each column, sixteen altogether, presenting scenes from the life of the saint and it is worth looking at each panel individually to get a sense of the story.

This series of panels tells the story of the Frideswide legend as Burne Jones saw it. He has taken liberties with her story, as have all of her legend-tellers but overall, it is a charming depiction of a historic figure.

Stained Glass in the Upper Tracery

Roundel

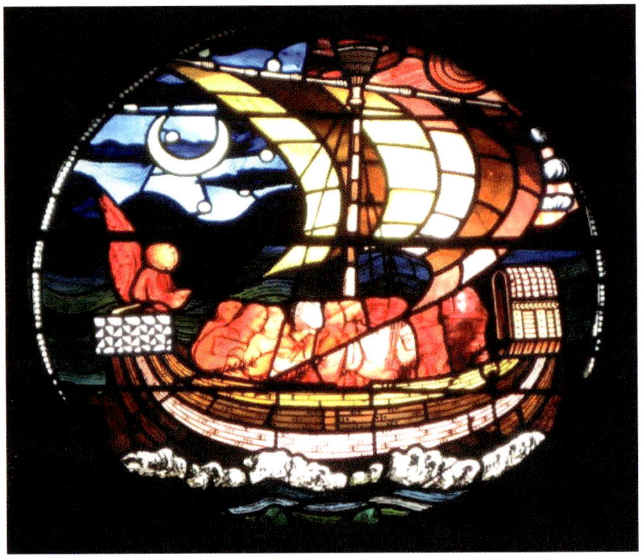

This roundel represents the ship of souls being taken to heaven by an angel.

Tree of knowledge

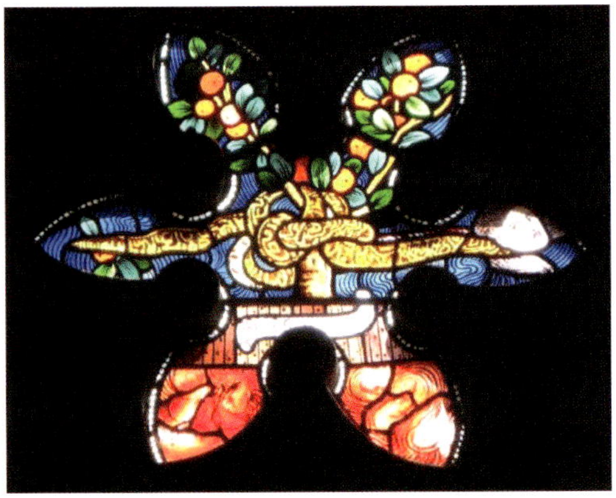

This is the tree in the garden of Eden whose fruit bought evil and death into the world.

Tree of Life

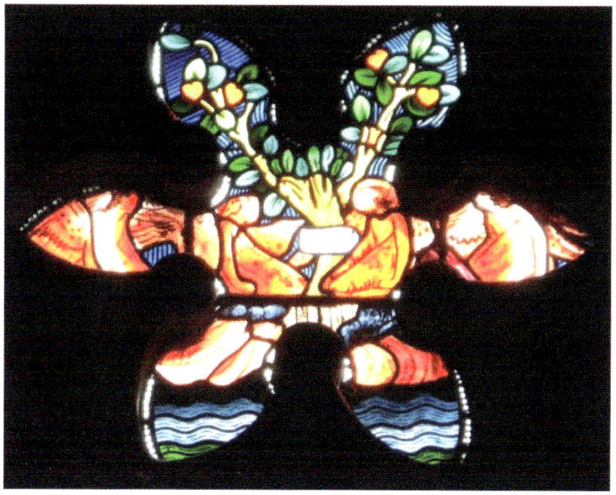

This is the tree in heaven whose fruit gives eternal life.

Sun, Moon, Stars

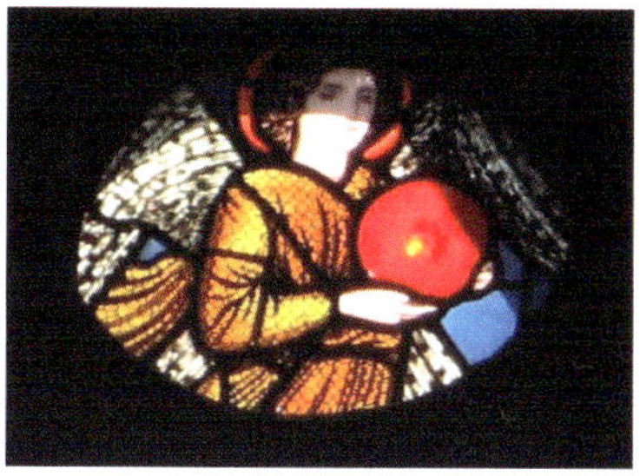

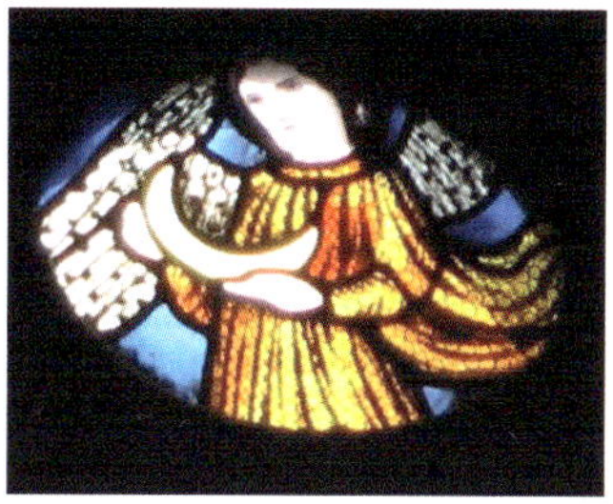

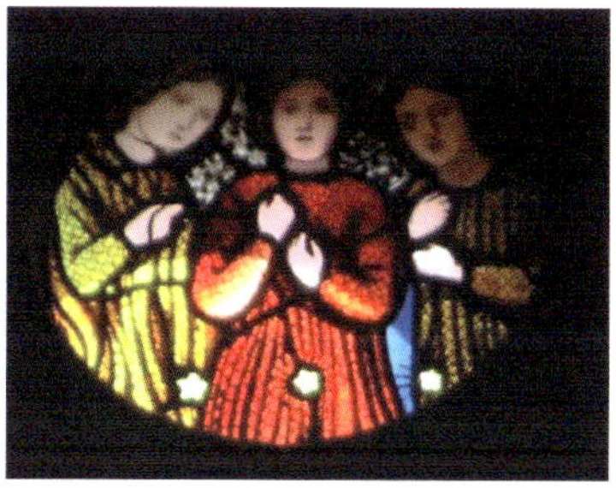

These are the heavenly objects vital for our existence.

Exterior of Latin Chapel

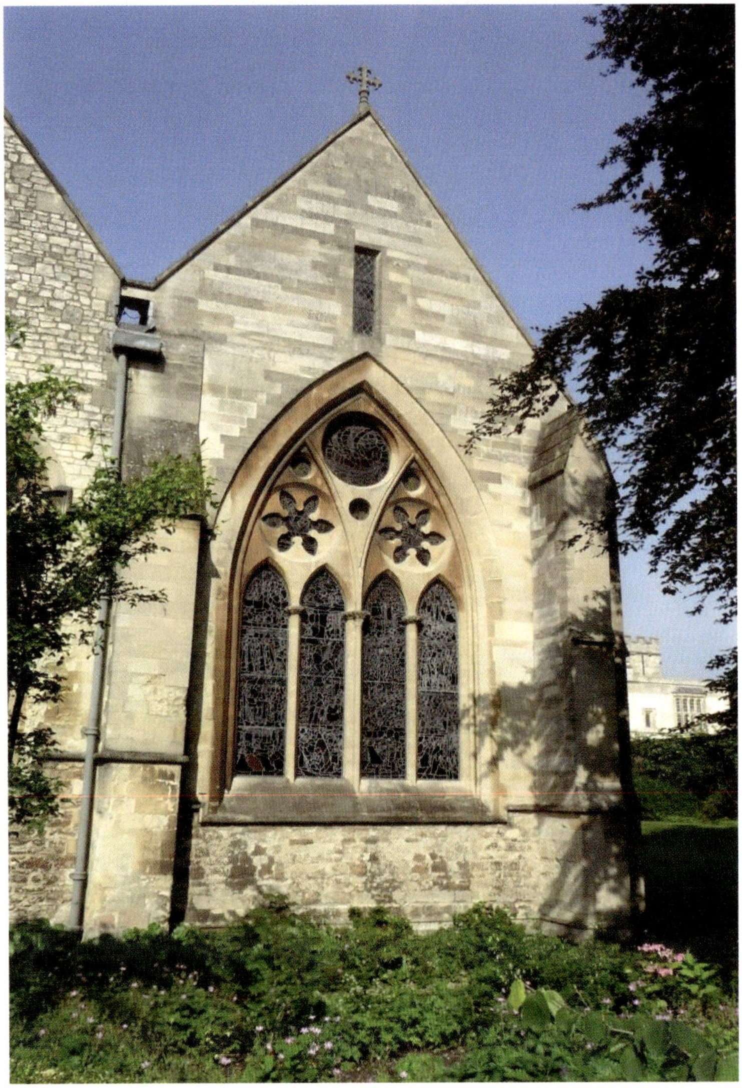

This photograph shows the exterior of the Frideswide window at the east end of the Latin chapel. The stonework above and around the window looks as though it has been renewed, while the stonework below looks original to the 14th century structure. Burne Jones himself designed the tracery with the large roundel and two petal shaped lights. It catches the sun in the mornings sending pools of coloured light onto the floor of the Latin chapel.

The Window Columns
and panels

Column One

Panel 1: The childhood of Frideswide.
Panel 2: Frideswide chooses to live for God.
Panel 3: King Algar sends a proposal of marriage.
Panel 4: Algar's men come to take Frideswide.

Column Two

Panel 1: Frideswide leaves Oxford.
Panel 2: King Algar is angry.
Panel 3: Frideswide hides in the forest.
Panel 4: Frideswide finds a place of safety.

Column Three

Panel 1: Frideswide escapes on the river.
Panel 2: King Algar pursues Frideswide.
Panel 3: Frideswide builds a chapel.
Panel 4: Frideswide prays for healing.

Column Four

Panel 1: God provides a well for the nuns.
Panel 2: Frideswide is chased back to Oxford.
Panel 3: King Algar is struck blind.
Pane 4: Frideswide dies.

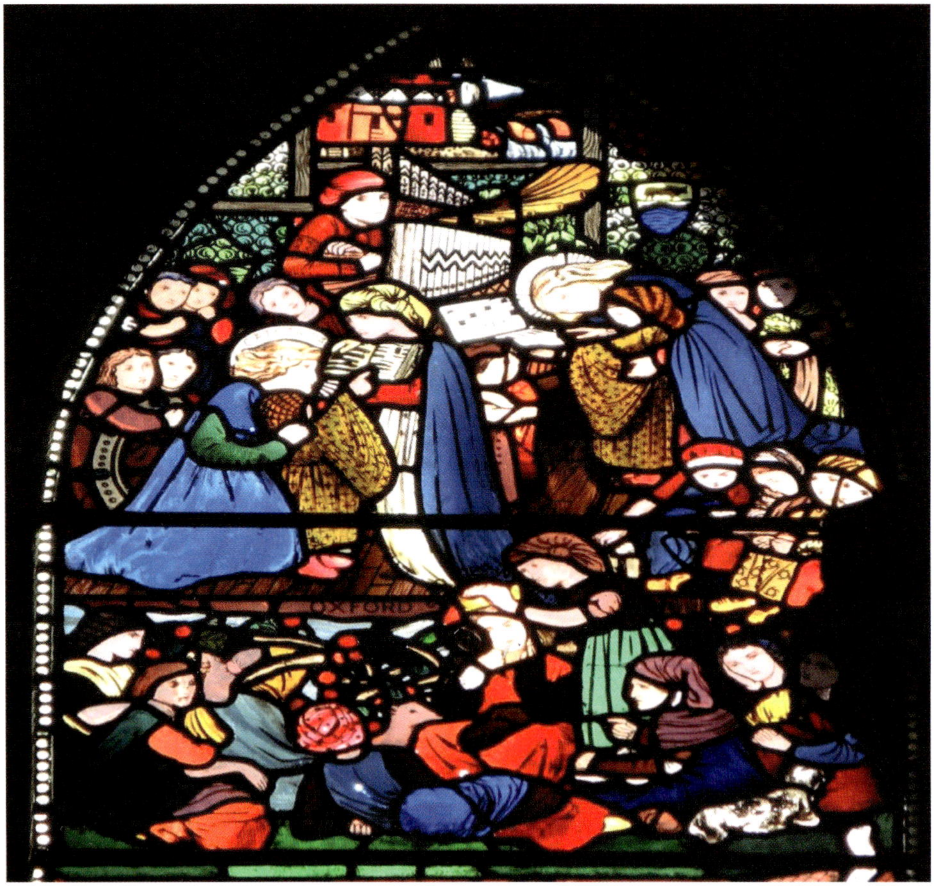

Column One: Panel One

The childhood of Frideswide.

This is a very full panel with several things happening at once. Frideswide is the little figure just to left of centre, between the two figures in blue. She is wearing a mustard dress with big sleeves and a pattern of crosses on the fabric. Her red boots are just visible, and she is pointing upwards to a book. Above the head of the kneeling figure is a halo with the word CATHARINA. This is Saint Catherine teaching Frideswide to read. Below these figures is the word OXFORD. In the second cameo, to the right just above centre, Frideswide has her hand on a set of piano keys with a piece of music and the word AMEN in front of her. A figure in a blue cloak is leaning over her, but the name on her halo is very faint. It is Saint Cecilia, teaching Frideswide to play. The ranks of pipes above the keys, and the gold seashell of trumpets, suggest it is a pipe-organ.

Above Saint Cecilia is the badge of Oxford, the Ox over Water, and at the very top of the panel is a depiction of the buildings of Oxford. At the bottom of the panel is a figure in red sitting cross-legged with what looks like a red and yellow halo being placed on her head by the woman in a green skirt. This must be Frideswide with her friends. In the middle of the bottom section is the head of a small pink animal like a deer and in the bottom right corner is a little dog.

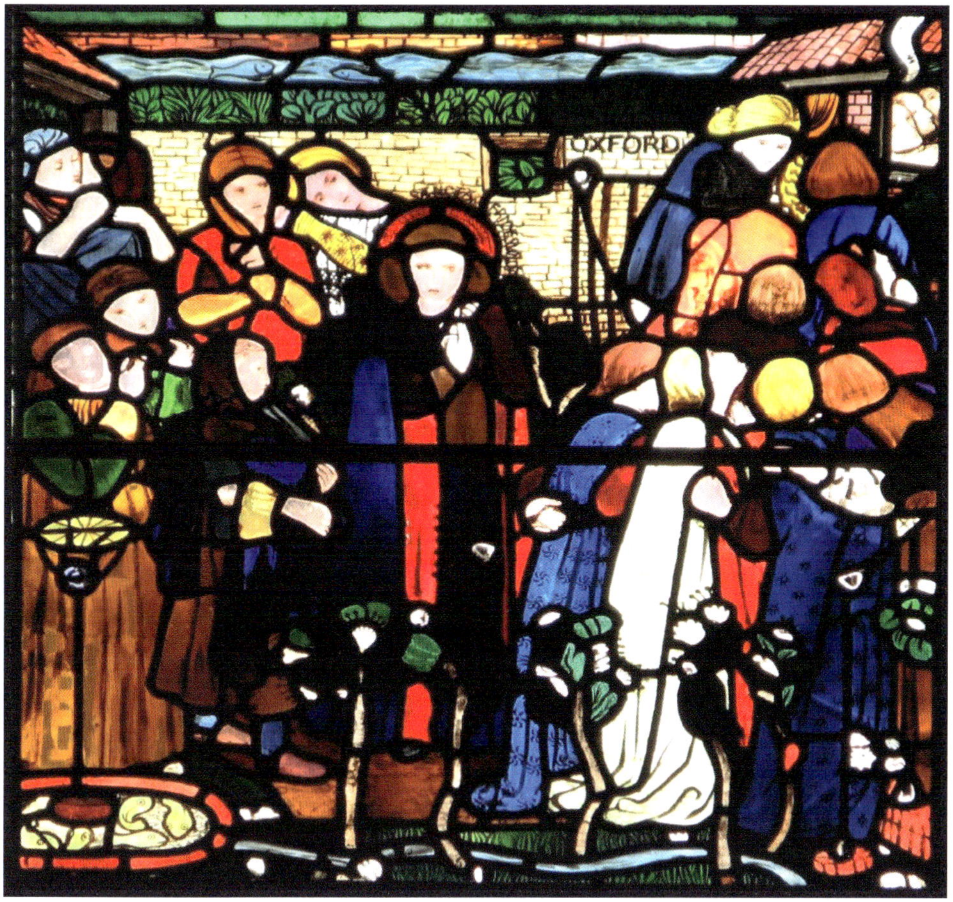

Column One: Panel Two

Frideswide chooses to live for God.

Frideswide is depicted as a central figure with a red halo in this panel. On the left are several figures looking downcast, and two figures on the top left are hugging each other. These are Frideswide's friends and family saying good-bye to her. On the right are several figures with their backs to the viewer entering a building. There are nine outside and two inside and, with the last figure hugging and saying good-bye on the left, these make up the twelve companions Frideswide took with her into the nunnery.

Behind her is a pale wall with the word Oxford and above that is greenery and the blue wavy line of a river, the Thames, suggesting she is inside the walls of Oxford. She is leaving a building on the top left, her home, and entering a building with a red-tiled roof on the right which is her nunnery. Against the wall are the black lines of a metal gate with a strap being held by a person on the right.

At the bottom left of the panel is a basket of fish and across the bottom runs a thin, wavy strip of water, possibly representing the Trill Mill Stream, that used to flow just outside her nunnery under the Broad Walk of Christ Church Meadow. There are flowering plants on long stalks and a lamp on a long shaft above the basket of fish.

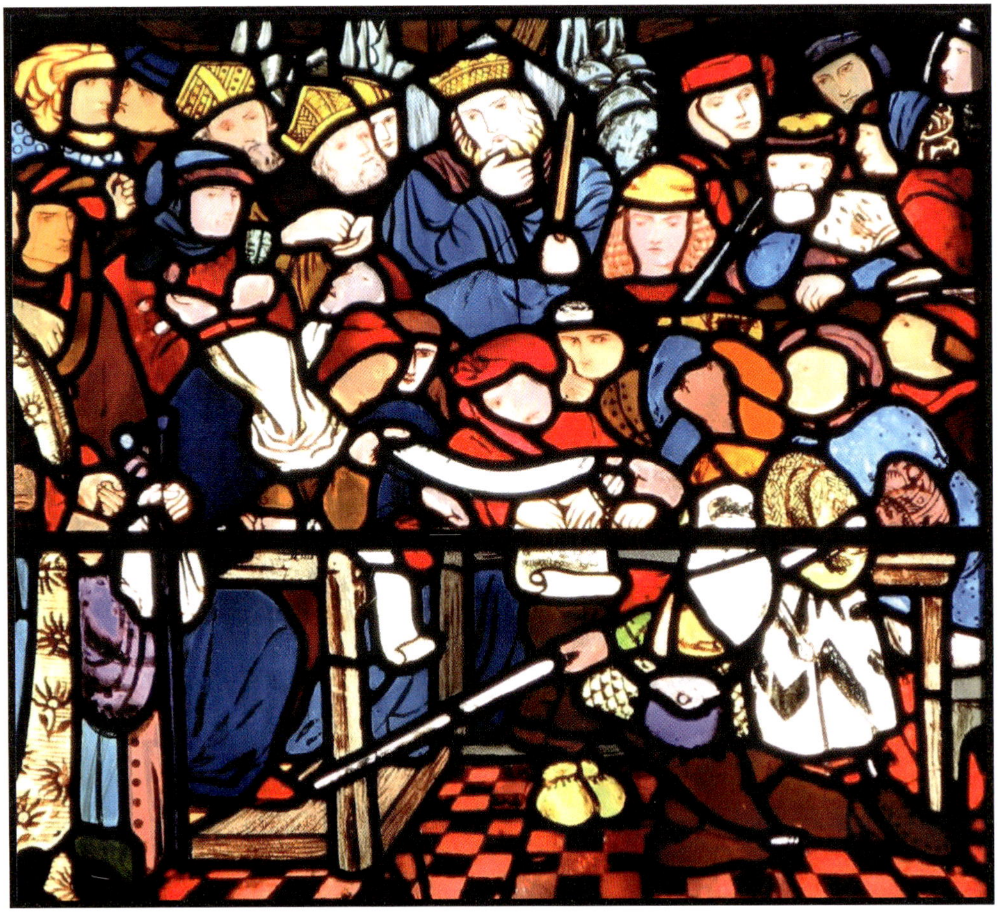

Column One: Panel Three

King Algar sends a proposal of marriage.

This panel is dominated by the bearded figure of a king in the top centre. Dressed in blue, he holds a rod in his left hand, while he ponders. On the top left are three men in mitres, probably bishops, and on the top right several well-dressed men who are probably his earls and nobles. On the left of the panel stand three beautifully dressed men holding things in their hands: these might be lawyers.

Standing, or half-sitting on a wooden platform in the centre of the panel is a man in blue with white sleeves, probably the king's secretary, who is poring over a white document held out to him by a man, kneeling on the right. This is Algar's messenger offering the marriage proposal to Frideswide's father, King Dydan, through his secretary. His yellow draw-string money bags suggests he is offering a dowry. Also note his leather boots, straw hat and lilac bag. He might have travelled some distance. Under his arm is a long white rod with its ornate head behind his back.

Around and about are many figures, and one in the centre is holding an open roll of parchment and appears to be reading the message from King Algar with his head on one side. The floor has red and black quarry tiles and behind the king are men in armour holding pikes or javelins. There is obviously some debate going on.

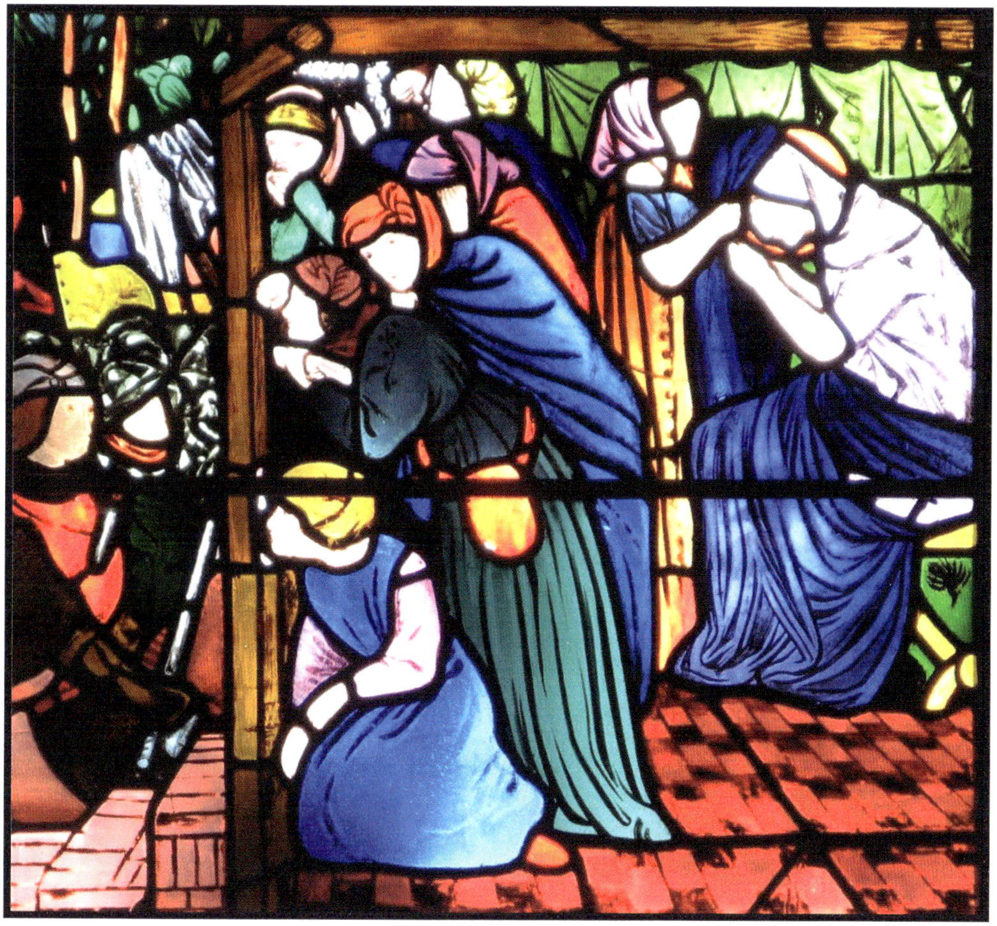

Column One: Panel Four

Algar's men come to take Frideswide.

The main feature of this panel is a large wooden structure, which is the nunnery, into which we can look. The nuns are dressed in brightly coloured garments, not in habits, which were not worn until much later in the Middle Ages. They are peering through the doors and windows, listening to the soldiers who are demanding to see Frideswide. She is seated on a crossed-legged stool at the right of the panel. She is distressed, refusing to go with Algar, and one of the nuns is with her, helping to put a blue garment over her head. There are green curtains hung behind her and black and red quarry tiles on the floor.

Outside, beyond the brick steps, one soldier, possibly King Algar himself, has his sword against the door and a dagger tucked in at his chest. He has other soldiers with him as can be seen by their helmets, visible above his companion. Above their heads is a waving yellow banner and several spears.

King Algar and his men have come to take Frideswide by force. The nuns are telling them that Frideswide does not consent to the marriage, but Algar is looking threatening as he attempts to intrude on the peaceful community and carry away their abbess.

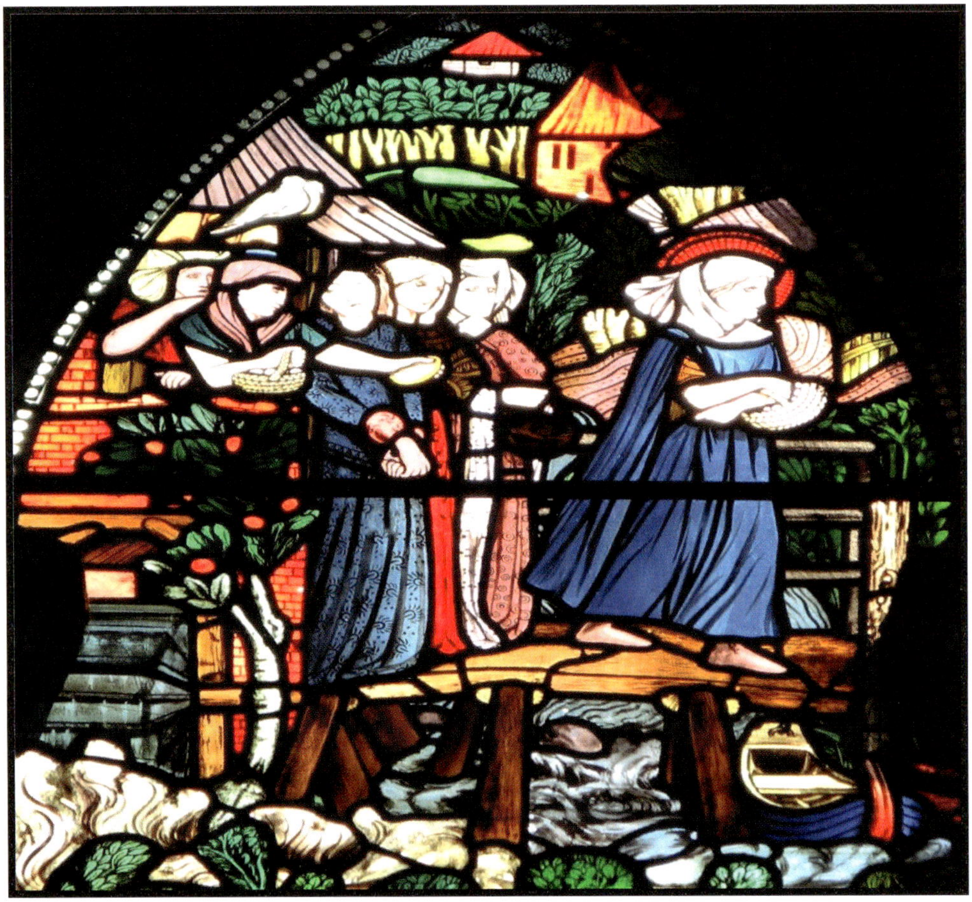

Column Two: Panel One

Frideswide leaves Oxford.

In the top panel of the second column, Frideswide is the figure in a blue dress crossing a wooden bridge. It has wooden railings just visible, which are held by wooden uprights. Below is a stream or river that is flowing fast through rapids and on the right is a small boat. She is holding a wicker basket and has a red halo, which is used throughout the panels to indicate her status as a saint.

In the top arch of the panel are the houses and gardens of Oxford. On the left are a group of nuns. One holds out a loaf of bread and a basket of eggs and above their heads are two white doves. Frideswide is leaving Oxford, her nunnery, and her companions, in great haste to escape on the river in the boat. The concerned faces of the women are touching.

On the left below the nuns is a brick wall and a water wheel, suggesting a mill, with a tree beside it bearing red fruit. At the bottom left of the panel are rocks and vegetation on the banks of the river. Frideswide's nunnery was very close to a branch of the river and the present Trill Mill Stream runs near the western edge of the nunnery's enclosure. Archaeologists have found evidence of alterations to its banks dating from the Anglo-Saxon period, and it certainly had a water mill at a later date.

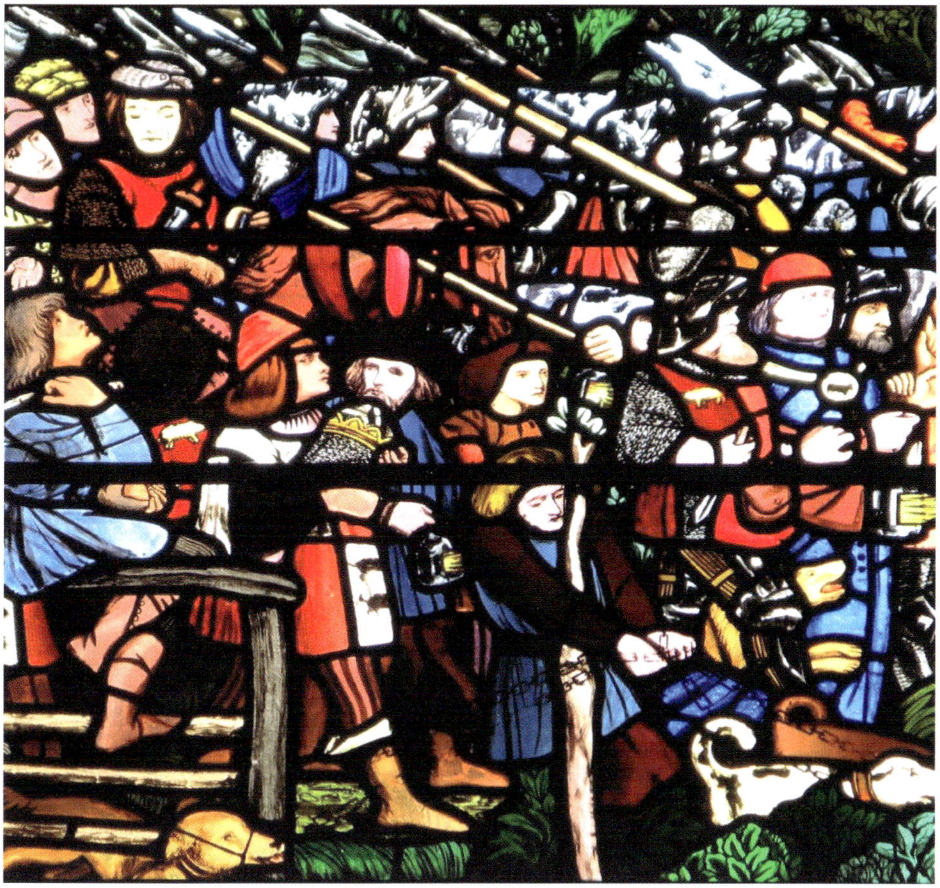

Column Two: Panel Two

King Algar is angry.

This panel is exceptionally busy and difficult to interpret even close-up. It is filled with a mass of men and weapons moving from left to right of the panel. King Algar is the prominent man on the top left. He is haughty, refusing to take 'No' from Frideswide and is riding a horse. He has a dagger on his chest and carries a lighted fire-torch in his left hand. Many soldiers in helmets stream across the top of the panel holding spears with metal blades across their figures.

In the left foreground is a boy in blue sitting on a fence and a man in red striped stockings and a coloured tunic decorated with the Ox of Oxenford. He is looking very smart and must be an official. He is carrying Algar's helmet, while his companion carries a lighted lantern. There are several dogs in the foreground. On the right is a man's face with a red cap. He is clad in blue with a white band around his shoulders carrying the badge of Oxford and might possibly be the mayor. He looks unhappy as though he has no wish to be helping them, but a soldier is holding him on either side, marching him along. One has the symbol of a white boar on a red ground, which is also on Algar's horse regalia. Perhaps Algar is making the mayor responsible for finding Frideswide?

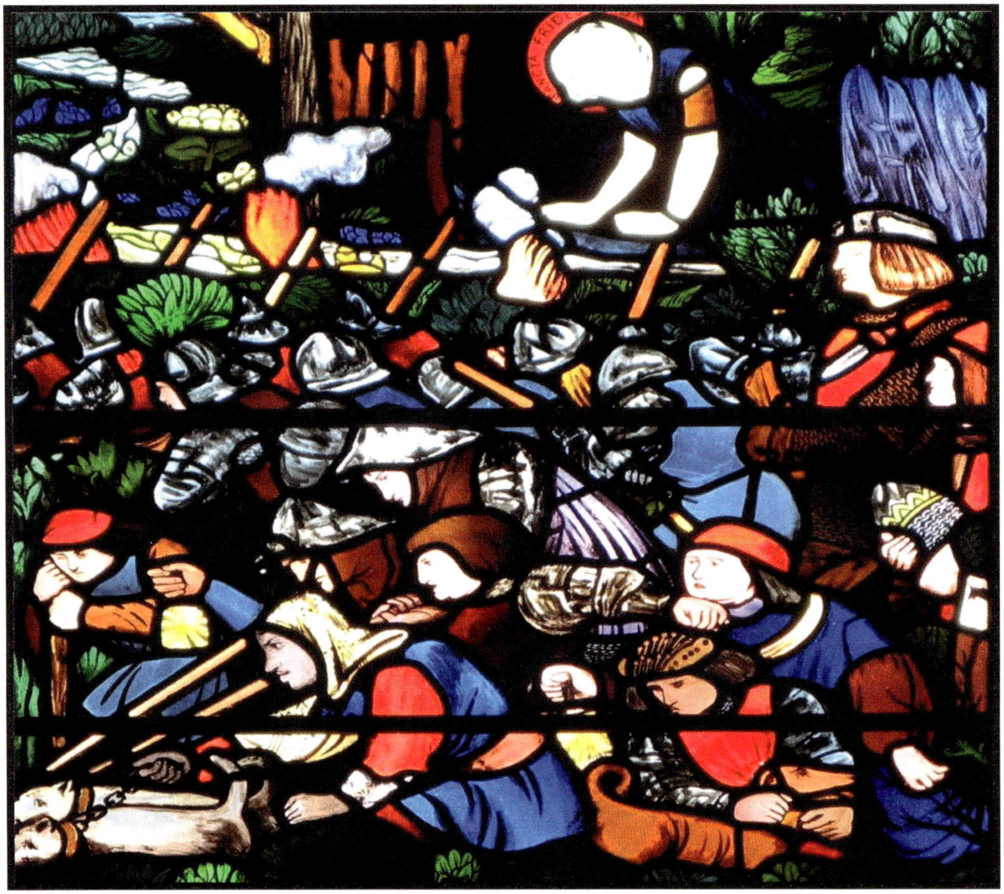

Column Two: Panel Three

Frideswide hides in the forest.

The soldiers are back, this time travelling from right to left of the panel, accompanied by men and dogs who are bending to search under bushes and between trees, looking for Frideswide. They know she is in the wood but cannot find her. It makes you want you call, 'She's behind you,' if we were not so concerned for the safety of this holy lady, who is being brutally hunted down with dogs and weapons, at the insistence of a rapacious king.

Frideswide is hiding at the top right, screened by greenery, in what looks like a wooden structure just to her left, but the blue blades of lances are positioned near her on the right. The soldiers in front of her are carrying poles, and flaming torches issuing smoke. The long strip of river is between them. King Algar is the haughty figure on the right, with his dagger on his breast, and his companion is still carrying his helmet. Two of the men in the foreground are carry lights and the large blue-clad figure of the mayor is at the bottom right, being dragged along and looking anxious.

The dogs are sniffing around; the soldiers are pushing their spears into every dark corner. It is only prayer that can save Frideswide now!

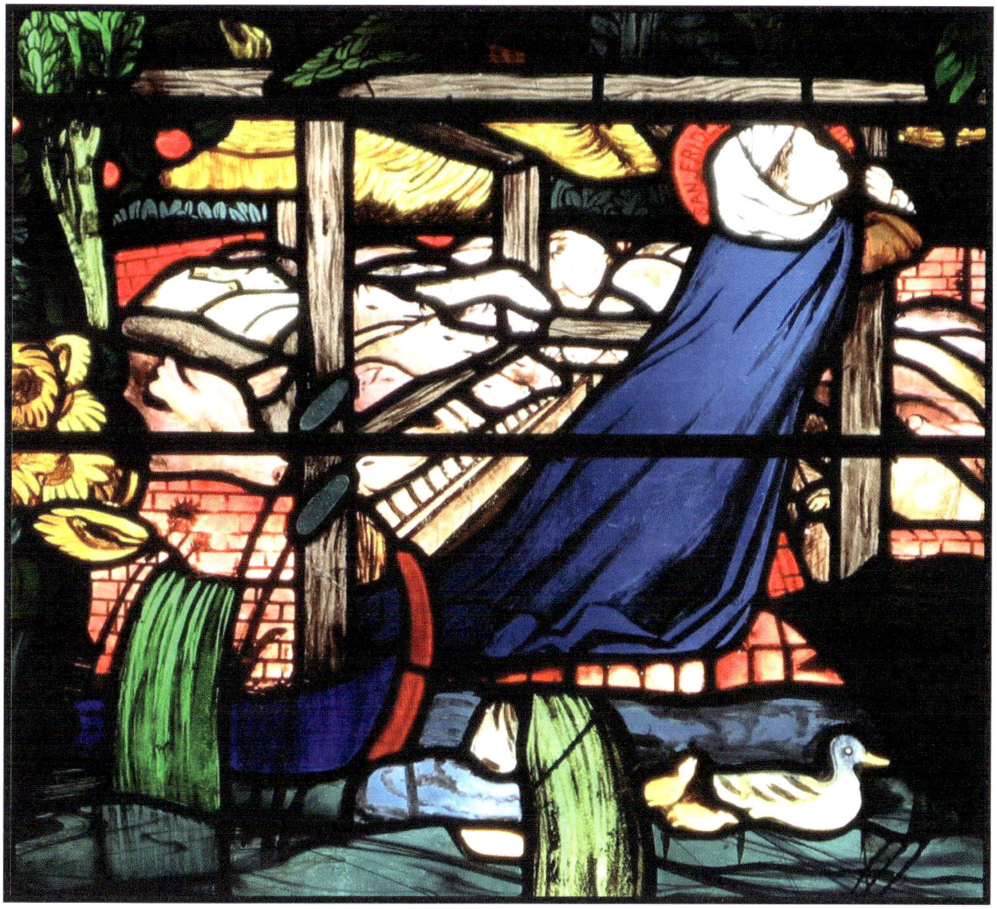

Column Two: Panel Four

Frideswide finds a place of safety.

Prayer is the only thing that Frideswide can do. She has found a pigsty and the pigs are asleep all around her while she leans against the post in exhaustion and directs her prayers to God. The soldiers are absent, having perhaps been temporarily foiled of their prey.

The pigs are lying in feeding stalls on either side of Frideswide, and the wooden super-structure of the pigsty is built on red-brick walls with a yellow thatched roof, and a red-brick floor: quite a substantial building. At the bottom of the panel is the river with a duck and ducklings peacefully unaware that Frideswide is afraid for her life and her virtue. The prominent blue of Frideswide's cloak, usually associated with the Virgin Mary, proclaims her virginity, and FRIDESWIDE around her red halo proclaims her identity.

A bright yellow clump of sunflowers brightens up the left side of the panel with a tree above bearing red round fruits, while tall green grasses and bulrushes grow out of the riverbanks. Her little blue boat with its curved, red prow is pulled up at the front on the left alongside the pigsty, hiding among the bulrushes. The pigsty is not mentioned in the earliest and most authentic legend, but it is described in later accounts of the legend.

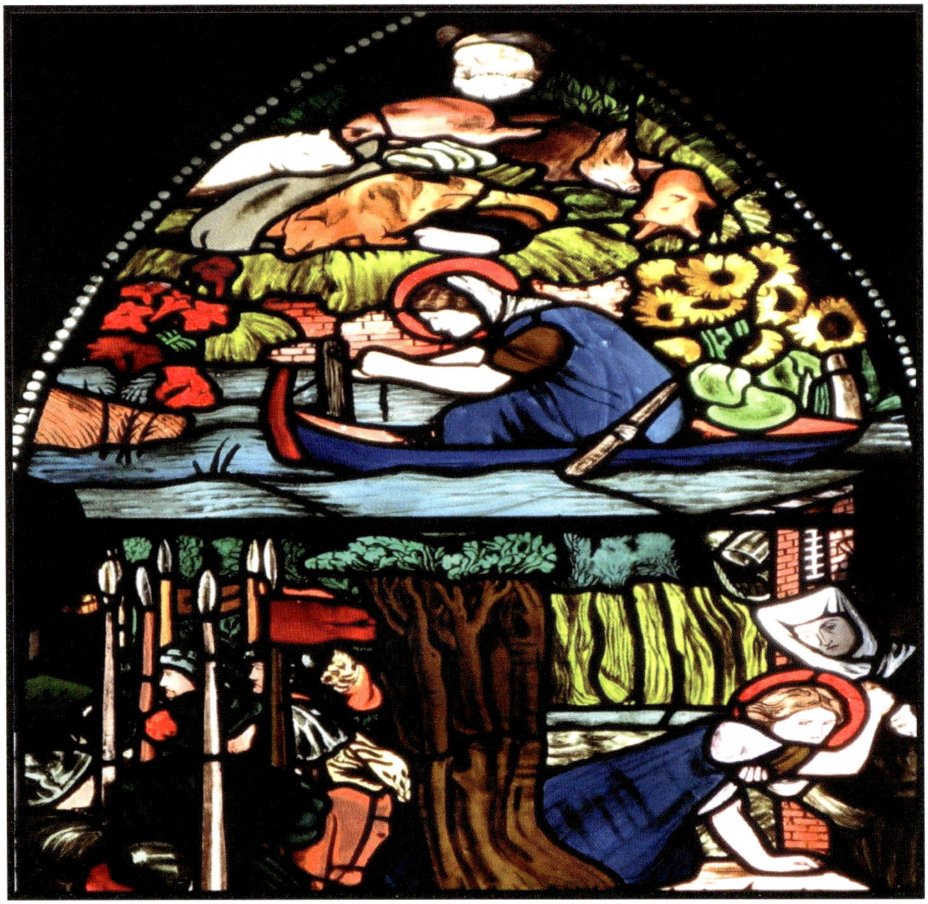

Column Three: Panel One

Frideswide escapes on the river.

Frideswide is on the move again. The panel is in two parts. In the top section Frideswide is back in her boat, untying it from the bank outside the pigsty, ready to cast off for a further trip on the river. She obviously does not feel safe where she is and leaves behind the sleeping pigs, the golden sunflowers, and the red water lilies in search of a better place.

The bottom section reveals why she is worried: she has heard the soldiers sneaking through the woods with their spears held upright and with red flags flying, still searching for her. The head of Algar's horse can just be seen at the middle of the bottom of the panel and the trees are glowing an eerie blue-green, perhaps in the moonlight. But somehow Frideswide eludes them and is seen on the bottom right being helped into a brick-built house by a nun. The doorbell, an actual bell above her head, it is still swinging from her frantic ringing. There was no record that Frideswide found refuge in another religious house, but the legend relates that she finally arrived at Binsey, today a small settlement over three kilometres north-west of the cathedral on the flood-plain of the river Thames, where she retreated a distance from the river into the wood with some of her nuns.

However, the nuns of Abingdon are known to have moved to Wytham in the late 7th century. Whether they had contact with Frideswide during her exile is unknown.

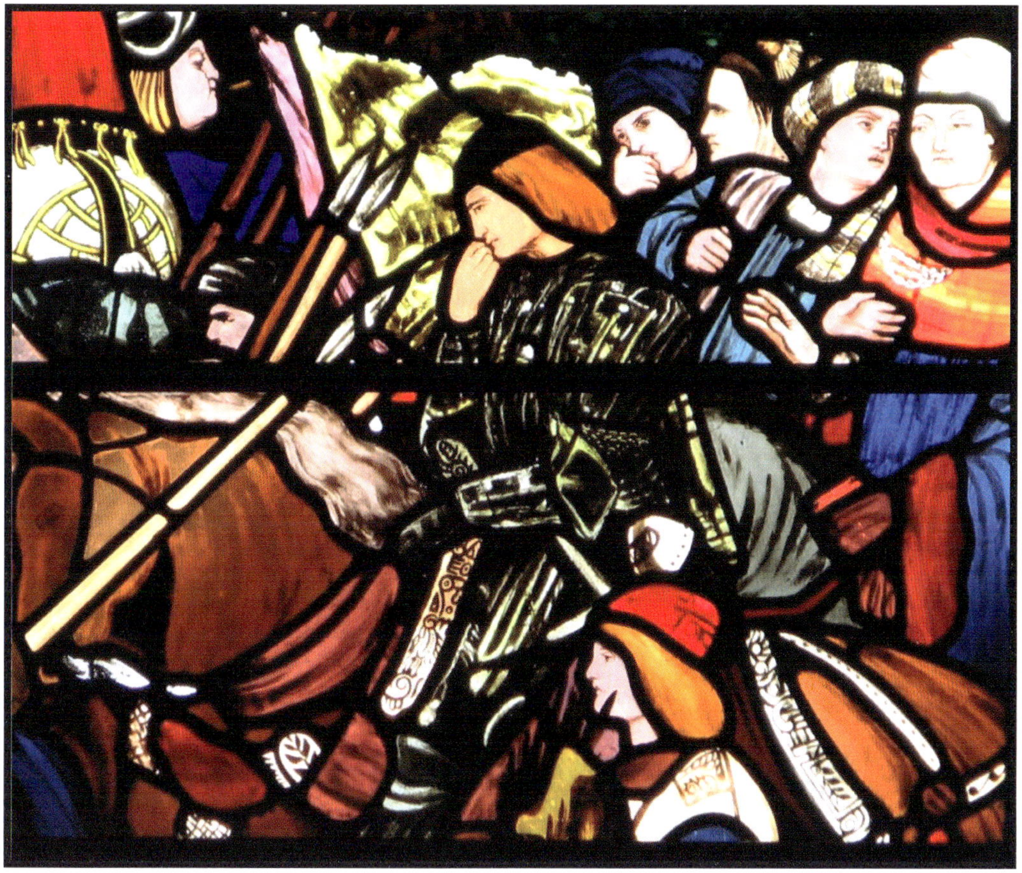

Column Three: Panel Two

King Algar pursues Frideswide.

Algar is revealed in his full regalia in this next panel. He is the central figure in armour on the back of his beautiful chestnut horse which is decorated with intricate metal straps and buckles as part of its regalia. Recent finds of beautiful Anglo-Saxon metal work suggest this is what might be expected on the horse of a king. He is surrounded by people, weapons, and flags. Behind him are four officials talking and arguing. The man on the right edge of the panel, with a metal chain across the orange cape on his chest, is riding a grey horse and, at his right hand, a man in a striped turban, is apparently warning him and trying to detain him with his hand. This official will have none of it, waving him aside to follow Algar.

Algar is looking thoughtful, perhaps contemplating how Frideswide has wronged him with her refusal. Next to his head are pink and yellow flags, and several spears held by foot soldiers. Ahead of him on the left, is the rump of a white horse with decorated gold braid-work over its flanks. Beside it, in the top left corner, is the face of a man blowing a bugle. The bugle is not shown here, but evident in the window. At the bottom of the picture is a man with a red hat, carrying a quiver full of arrows.

Frideswide had better watch out. This man is not giving up. He means business. But who would shoot arrows at a defenceless, holy lady?

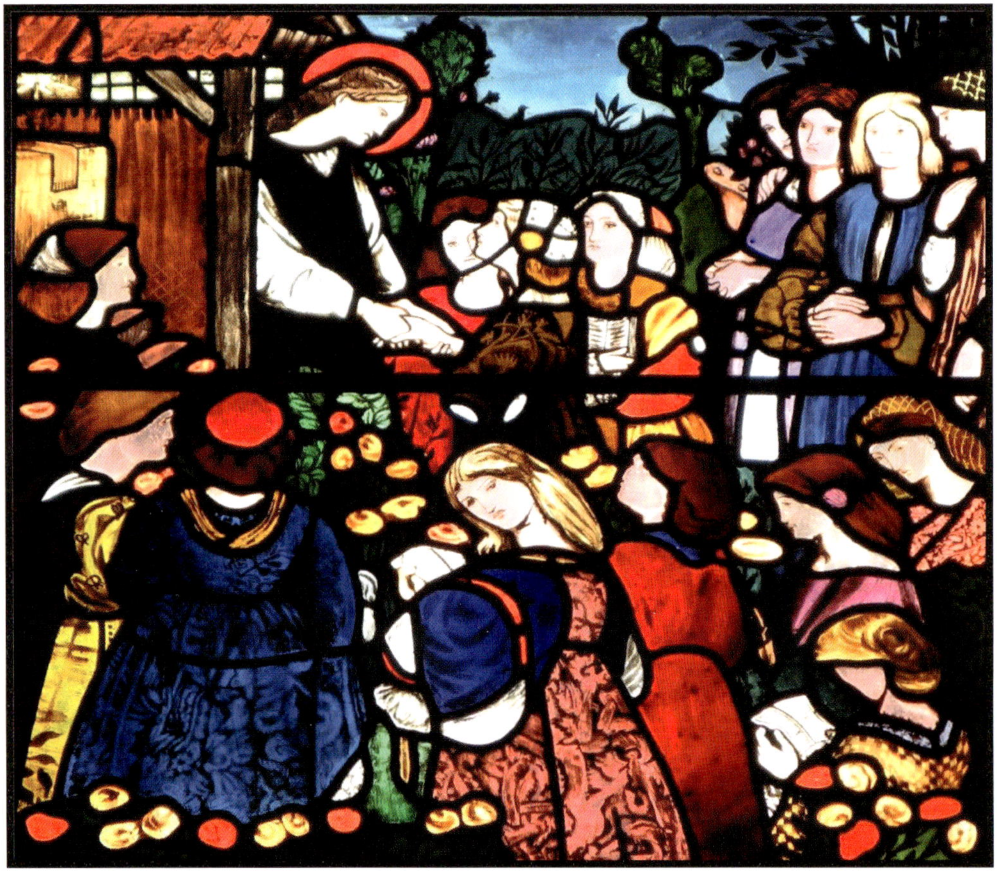

Column Three: Panel Three

Frideswide builds a chapel.

Frideswide has found a safe place in Binsey and has built an oratory (house of prayer) intending to stay for a while. In the top left of this panel is a wooden shelter with an open side, which enables us to see the altar, looking bright with a golden light. Frideswide is at the door holding the hand of a young girl who is being supported by two women. The legend records that a young girl who was blind, had a dream which led her to Frideswide. Frideswide bathed her eyes with water she had used to wash herself, and the awed look on the face of the girl shows her sight has returned.

The woman immediately behind the girl is holding what looks like an open book against her chest, possibly a Bible. The young woman with golden hair, looking towards the viewer at the bottom of the panel, is holding a cloth to dry the girl's eyes, and the woman at the bottom right is reading. While most figures appear female, the figure with a red hat and blue brocade coat on the bottom left of the panel appears to be an official and probably a man, or even the girl's father. Altogether there are twelve female figures, possibly the twelve nuns, as well as the mother of the girl. On the other hand, these may just be representatives of the local community of Binsey, or Seacourt, who would have been subsistence farmers on the flood-plain to the north of Oxford. There are many flowers dotted around and greenery from trees and woodland.

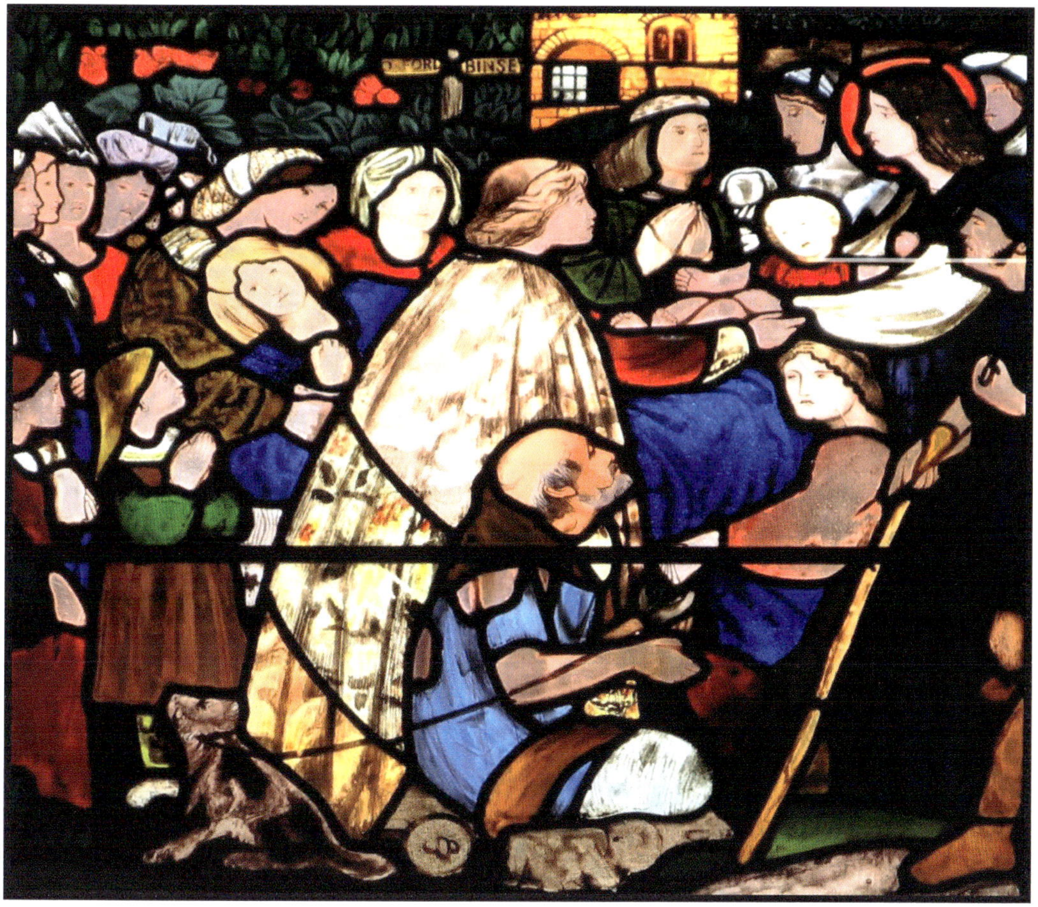

Column Three: Panel Four

Frideswide prays for healing.

This panel is again a scene at Binsey, as indicated by the signpost at the top-middle of the picture. The gold-lit building with the arched windows must be a more substantial oratory, or small church and suggests she has been there some time, possibly three years, as recorded in the legend. Frideswide is still surrounded by people who she is reaching out to help, as was characteristic of her.

Frideswide is holding a crying child, which its mother is offering, while behind the mother is a young girl lying on a long stretcher covered in a blue blanket and being supported by another woman. In the centre bottom of the panel is an old man with a bandaged stump of a leg, sitting on a little trolley. He is holding the lead of a shaggy, brown dog, with a bandaged paw, and he may represent the man with leprosy Frideswide is said to have healed with a kiss. The little girl on the left has her hands together as if in prayer and, half cut off by the right edge of the panel, is a man leaning for support on his stick. All the figures in this and other panels are beautifully rendered and very Pre-Raphaelite in their depiction.

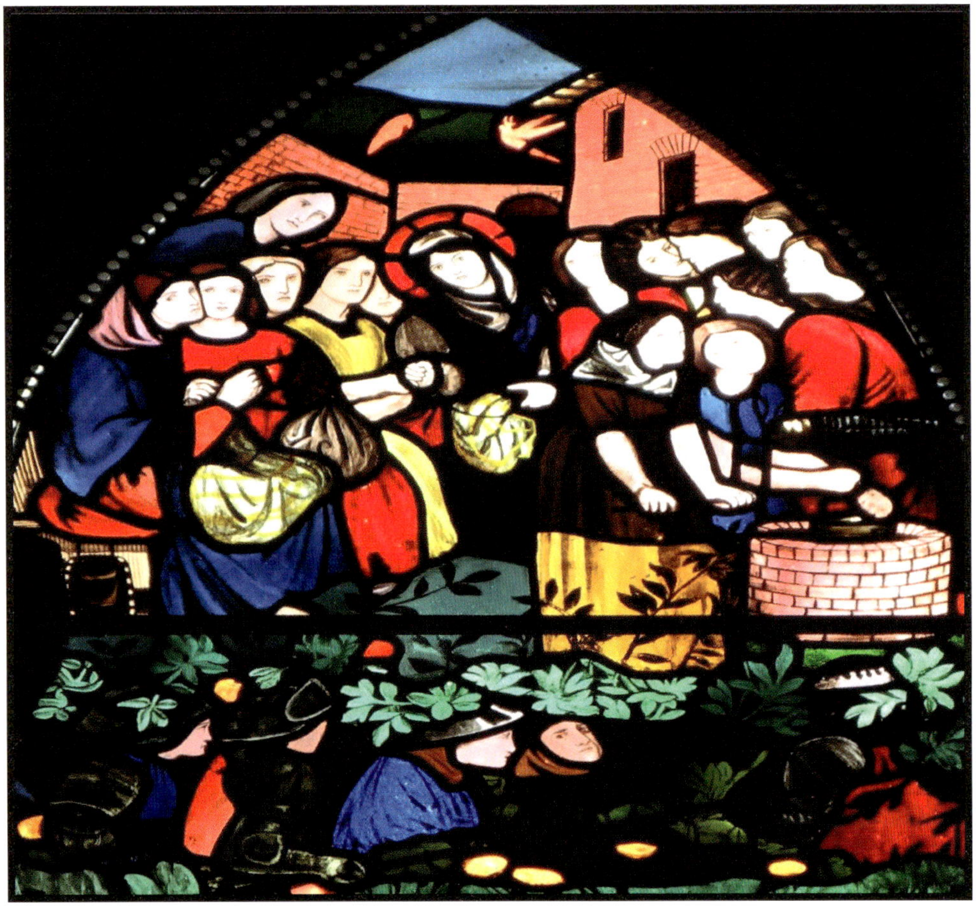

Column Four: Panel One

God provides a well for the nuns.

Column four starts with a placid scene of domesticity at Binsey, with doves flying over a much more substantial group of buildings. Frideswide is calmly sewing, surrounded by her twelve ladies, while two more are drawing water from the well. The legend records that the nuns had to go to the river Thames for water every day, and they complained to Frideswide at the distance. Even today the church at Binsey is about a kilometre by the road from the river. Frideswide prayed for water and a well of fresh, clear water miraculously appeared. Here it is depicted by a brick-built well where a nun is letting down a bucket for water.

St Margaret's Church, Binsey is located within an iron-age ditch, which was once surrounded by thorn trees, and the area was known a Thornbiri (or Thornbury today). There is still a spring (referred to as a well) in the ground to the west of the church. It is believed to be historically linked to healing miracles, tying in with the Frideswide legend of a sacred well, and the water is still fresh and clear despite its dark appearance. In the later Saxon period, Binsey was not the isolated place it is now, but on a well-trodden route from Wytham to Oxford which can still be traced today. One or two ladies are glancing sideways to where, at the bottom of the panel, soldiers are still scouring the hedgerows in search of Frideswide. She too appears to be aware of her danger, although seems serene.

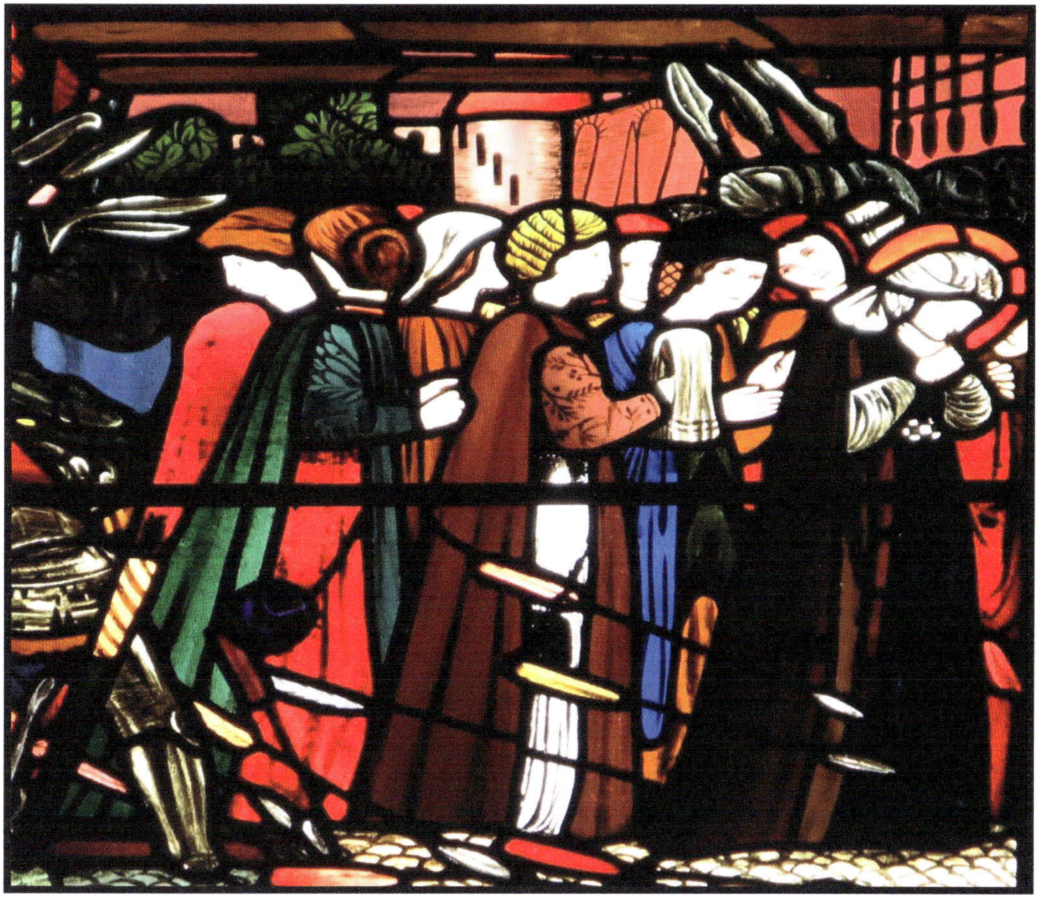

Column Four: Panel Two

Frideswide is chased back to Oxford.

Frideswide's peace at Binsey is suddenly shattered when Algar's men discover her hiding place, and this panel depicts her hurrying back through the gates of Oxford with Algar's arrows and spears in pursuit. Frideswide is the figure with the red halo on the right, holding her hands to her neck. She is upset and a nun behind is offering her a handkerchief for her tears. At least seven of her ladies are with her, several looking back at the soldiers. Two of the arrows appear to pierce Frideswide's cloak.

The scene seems to be taking place inside a structure, possibly the North Gate of Oxford, as wooden joists are visible at the top of the panel, and there are cobbles beneath their feet. Above Frideswide's head is a lifted portcullis and soldiers with spears are between them and the city walls in the background. One of the round bastions of the wall is clearly visible. Several spears are being poked at their heads from behind and an armour-clad soldier is bending down to the left of the panel. He is half cut off and it is not clear what he is doing, though two of the nuns are looking back at him. A quiver of arrows is slung across his back, and several arrows have fallen onto the cobbles. Of course, 8th century Oxford would have been too small to have a wall, and it was probably the north gate of the monastery enclosure that is described. King Algar is entering her own domain to try and kidnap her. He had better watch out.

It is a disturbing picture to imagine an innocent and holy nun being pursued in this way, but Frideswide's prayers of terror and distress are about to be answered.

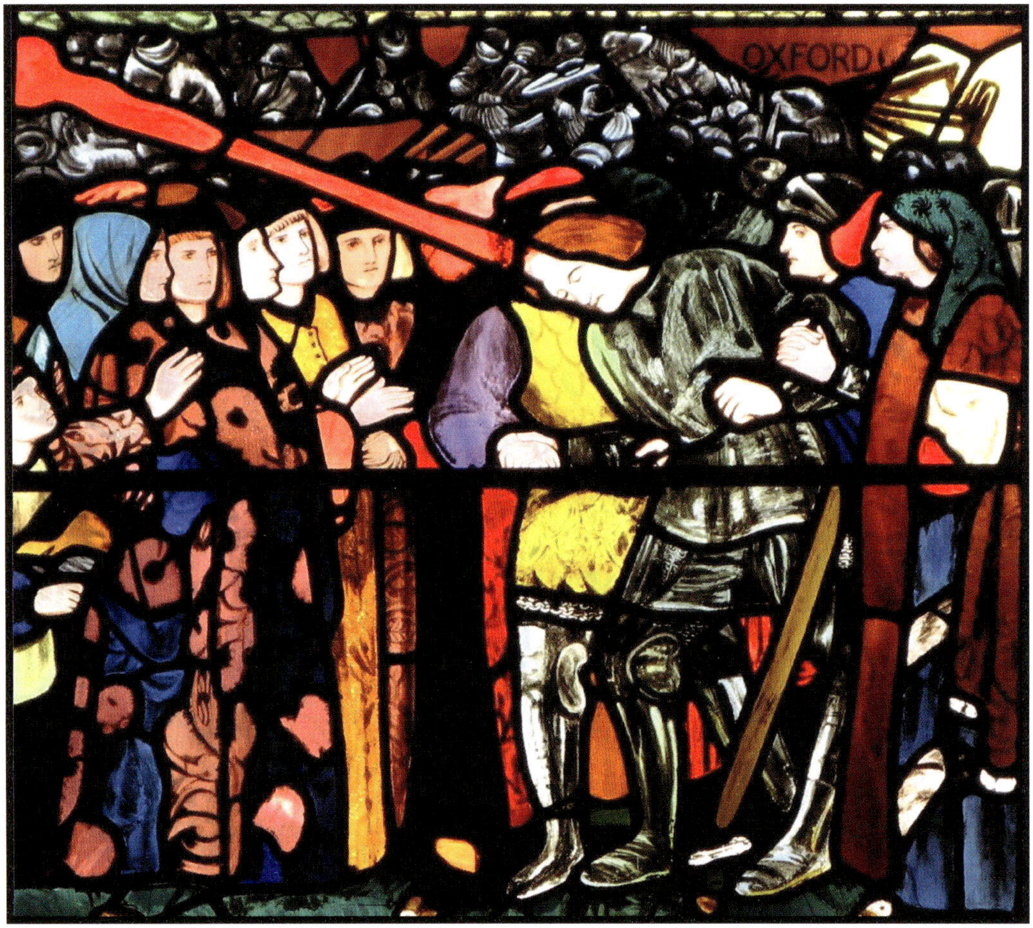

Column Four: Panel Three

King Algar is struck blind.

King Algar gets his just desserts in this penultimate panel. God has finally come to the aid of Frideswide and Algar is struck by a thunderbolt from heaven. Losing his eyesight and about to fall, he is having to be held upright by two of his men. He is being observed by the officials of Oxford, some of whom are holding up their hands in horror, some of whom are just stunned by what has happened. A jumble of armour, helmets, and weapons at the top of the panel suggest his soldiers are in disarray.

The legend has two versions of the outcome. Both versions state that he was struck blind, but do not mention a thunderbolt, which Burne Jones has used with artistic licence to depict the miracle. The earliest legend account suggests that he realised his wickedness, repented, and begged forgiveness, and Frideswide prayed for his sight to be returned. The later legends suggest he remained obdurate and stayed blind all his life, needing to be continually helped by other people and unrepentant of his wicked ways.

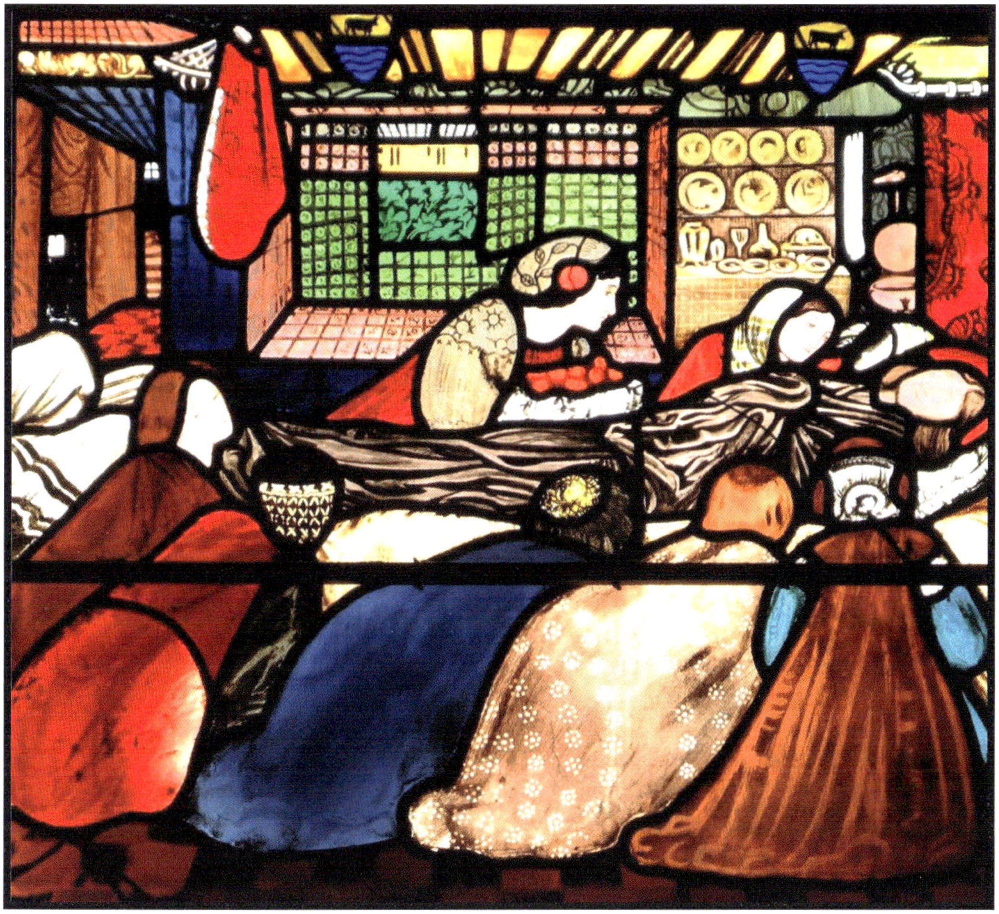

Column Four: Panel Four

Frideswide dies.

This is the saddest panel of the series. Frideswide has returned to her nunnery to live in peace and continue her life of prayer and good works, but she does eventually die. The later version of the legend describes a vision of saints and angels who come to take Frideswide to heaven, but Burne Jones shows it as a simple death scene where Frideswide is laid on her couch and her ladies kneel around her, mourning her passing. Their facial features still show sadness, though the stained glass has faded now with time.

Here Burne Jones has taken more liberties with the background, including many things familiar to a modern audience, including a Victorian dresser with a display of crockery. A flush toilet (a modern invention in 1858) is behind a brocade curtain, hanging from a curtain rail. The pebble-glass panels of the window with its deep embrasure, and the ornate wooden ceiling are also modern. Two distinct city badges of Oxford, the ox over the water, hang from the ceiling joists.

Her age at death is not recorded, but some historians assume Frideswide lived a full life span. However, as so little is known of her later life, another possibility is that she died young. No name has been found of any later abbess, so it may be that her monastery continued entirely on the memory of its charismatic founder, who inspired succeeding generations by the miracles that came with her prayers.

The Sunlit Interior of the Latin Chapel

Illuminating the 1289 shrine of St Frideswide

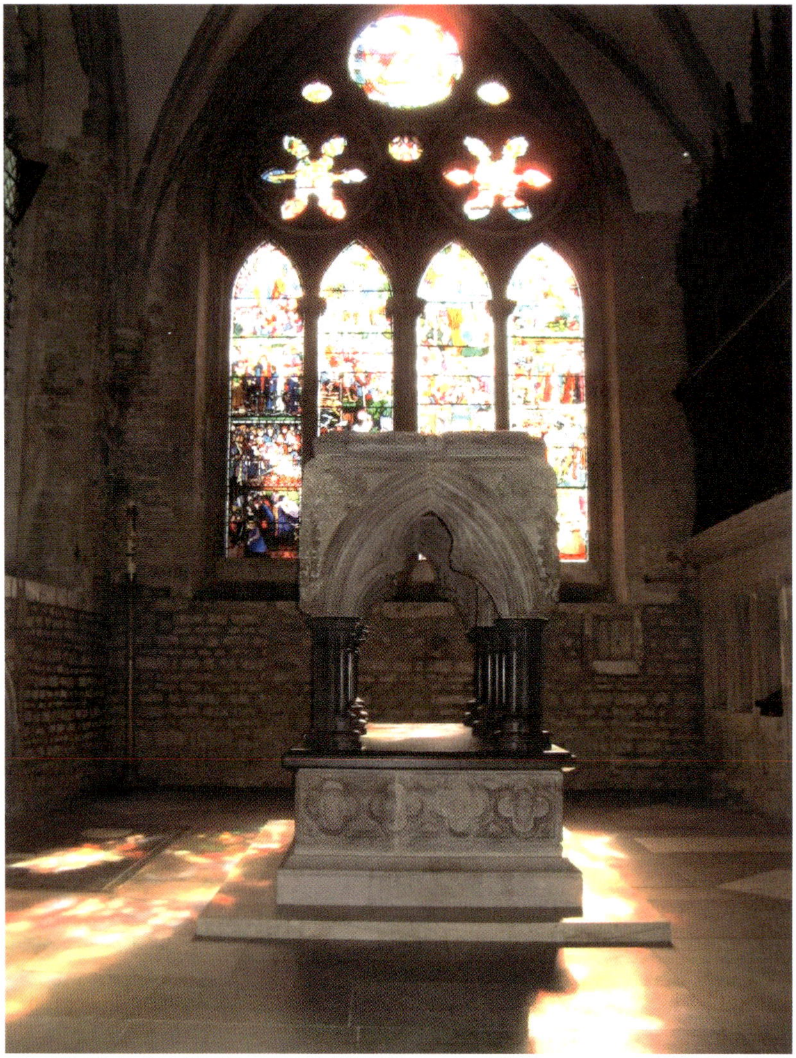

The 1289 shrine is illuminated by the morning sunlight and the floor of the chapel is bathed in multi-coloured light. The position of the shrine obscures access to the window making the window panels appear a mosaic of small shapes.

The story behind the window

A Saint and a City

The monastery of Saint Frideswide started as a little nunnery, led by Frideswide as abbess with twelve nuns chosen from her friends. It is believed to have followed the rule, which Frideswide instigated herself, of chastity, prayer and good works, but it did not remain in that form for very long after her death.

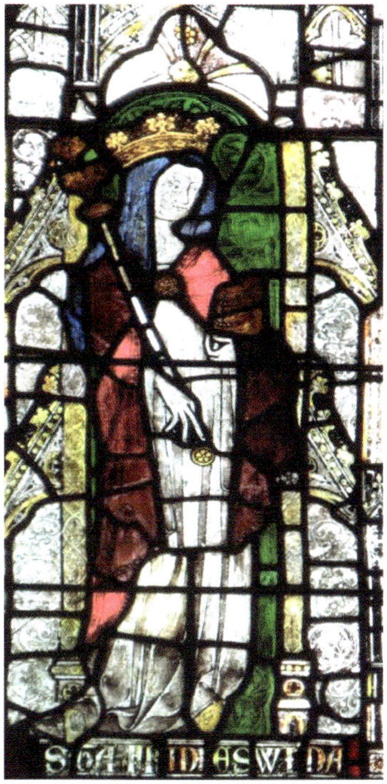

14th century depiction of St Frideswide

In subsequent centuries, it probably followed the course of many similar religious establishments and changed to a double monastery where the monks and nuns lived in adjacent houses. In time, the rise of secular Minsters alongside these early monasteries meant the nuns moved on while the role of the monks changed so that they acted more like the parish priests of today, able to marry and serve the needs of an extended community. They were known as Seculars, as opposed to Regulars who led a monastic life. Many Minsters had a network of satellite chapels in the surrounding villages, from which developed the present parish system.

But disaster was to come with the Viking attacks in the eighth to the eleventh centuries, which decimated monasteries all over England, culminating in the destruction of Saint Frideswide's monastery church on 13th November 1002. Known as the Brice Day Massacre, the church was burned to the ground by the townsfolk of Oxford in an attempt to eliminate the Danish settlers who had fled there for safety. This had been instigated by a decree of King Æthelred II (the Unready) and unfortunately, all the documents and records of the early monastery were lost in the fire.

It was only the remorse of King Æthelred that prevented Frideswide from vanishing, like so many Anglo-Saxon saints, as a wisp of vapour into the mists of time. Badly advised, possibly by Eadric Streona, a wicked earl of Oxford, Æthelred had given the command that led the people of England to turn against the Danes.

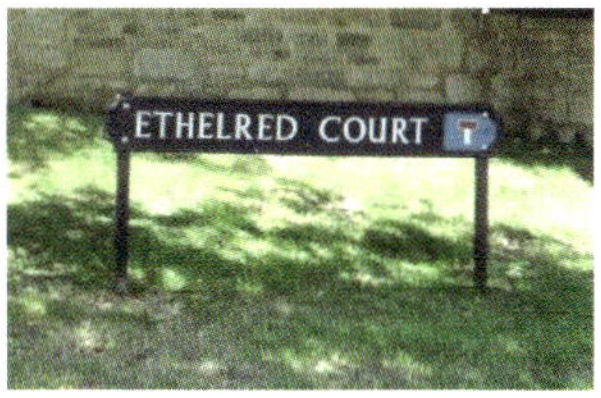

A modern road in Headington, Oxford, where Æthelred once had a palace.

There is little in history that suggests that other cities were affected, but Oxford was Streona's stronghold, and his influence may have made sure that Æthelred's command was carried out to its fullest extent.

However, the unfortunate desecration of a holy church, particularly one with an early English saint as a patron, led Æthelred to believe that his immortal soul was in danger.

The king was lavish in his remorse, and his 1004 foundation charter of the renewed church and monastery, shows how he believed in Frideswide's status as a saint, and regretted his actions. Yet, although he re-founded her monastery, rebuilt and enlarged her church and endowed it with new property and lands, the continued upheaval of the eleventh century, culminating in the Norman Conquest in 1066, made it impossible for a community that thrived on peace and seclusion to properly exist. The memory of this early saint might have been eliminated altogether if it had not been for the piety of the invaders.

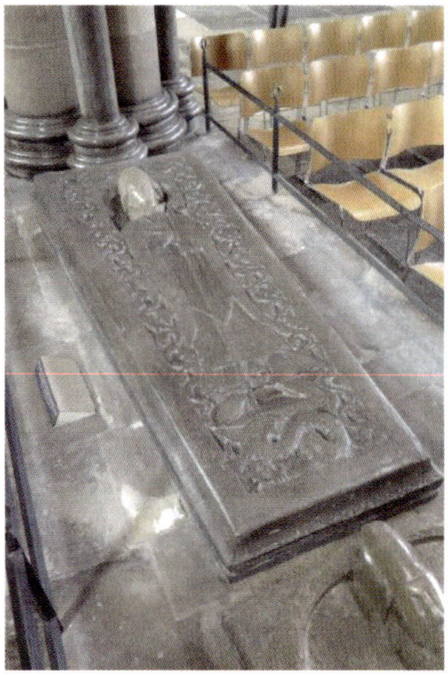

The tomb of Roger of Salisbury

As it happened the new Norman overlords were devout Christians, determined to revive the faltering flame of faith in England and they started with re-founding many of the old Anglo-Saxon monasteries. With an injection of money from influential patrons, and a boost of dedicated manpower, many were set back on track as religious houses, and Saint Frideswide's was no exception. It happened during the reign of Henry I, son of William the Conqueror, and Frideswide's rescuer was Roger, Bishop of Salisbury, an influential person who became no less than second in the land to the king.

In 1122, Roger of Salisbury re-founded Saint Frideswide's as an Augustinian priory with a prior and a contingent of canons (full-time monks with no parish commitments). Despite this, the Priory of Saint Frideswide at Oxford did not become as well-known as others founded around the same time, possibly because the saint had not been a prestigious or influential figure and was little known outside the Oxford area during her lifetime.

However, the far-sighted second prior, Robert of Cricklade, wanted to make the most of what he had, and he recognised the strength of the miracle stories that surrounded the early cult of Saint Frideswide. With the rediscovery of Christianity in twelfth-century England, he realised that prestige could be built up, and money could be made from the existence of Oxford's very own Anglo-Saxon saint. He would also have had an altruistic reason, as he had himself been cured of illness by a pilgrimage to the grave of Thomas à Becket, who had been martyred in 1170. Monasteries were the only places which could provide care for the sick and infirm, and the presence of a miracle-working saint was invaluable.

To boost the position and influence of the new priory, he had already begun, in around 1150-1170, to build a new church in her honour. This building, completed in the early 13th century, still stands as the Anglican Cathedral of the Diocese of Oxford, and is the building we know and love today. He then attempted to popularise Saint Frideswide with the re-discovery of her grave and the construction of a fabulous, bejewelled shrine to take her relics. He perfectly judged the local mood with a wonderful ceremony on 12th February 1180, presided over by the third prior, Philip of Oxford, and attended by many bishops, prelates, and other religious dignitaries. The representative of the Pope (Pope's legate) was also in attendance. Frideswide's cult was firmly established when over a hundred miracles occurred at her shrine, meticulously recorded by the third prior, who saw them all first-hand.

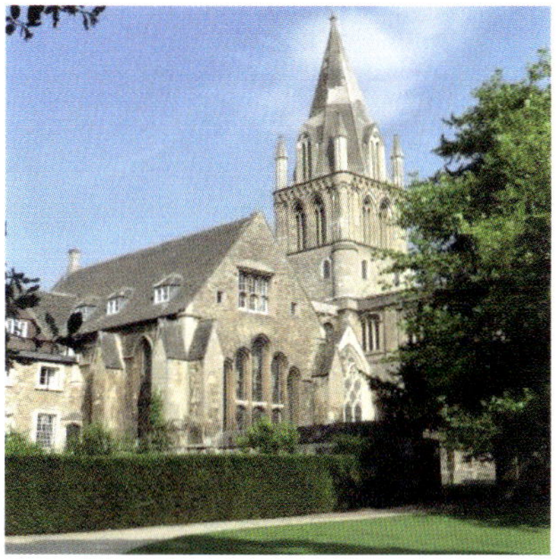

Christ Church Cathedral from the garden

The crossroads at Carfax has been dated to the 8th century, and the streets of the city were laid out as early as the tenth century. There was a main north-south route (now Woodstock Road, Cornmarket and St Aldates), running right past the priory and connecting the Midlands with the south coast, and an east-west route (now High St and Queen Street) connecting London with the west, in particular, the troublesome Welsh borders. It was defended by an Anglo-Saxon motte and bailey castle, possibly constructed in the early tenth century by Æthelflaeda of the Mercians (the daughter of Alfred the Great) and her husband, the Mercian overlord Ethelred, as part of a string of defences against the Vikings.

The first city defences, an earth bank surmounted by a wooden palisade, dated to King Offa in the 8th century, and were reinforced by King Edward the Elder (brother of Æthelflaeda) in the early 10th century. The town church of St Martin's, of which the tower at Carfax is the only part remaining, was built in the early eleventh century, probably on the site of an earlier Saxon church, and meetings of the town council were held in its churchyard.

By the eleventh century, Oxford was a significant metropolis, strategically placed, well defended, visited by the Saxon kings of England and host to several meetings of parliament. It was not far behind London itself in importance, though after the Conquest it fell back in size and prestige.

In 1129, it acquired a second monastery when Oseney Abbey, founded by Ethel the wife of Robert d'Oligi, the constable of Oxford Castle, was built. It was the rivalry between the two great religious houses of St Frideswide and Oseney, along with the court cases that ensued, that might be credited with the foundation of the University we have today. It brought the great and good from the religious and legal worlds of the Middle Ages, to Oxford to study and debate Canon Law, along with their followers and students.

Not only that, the great new abbey and the ancient priory, along with the early students, brought in further religious houses

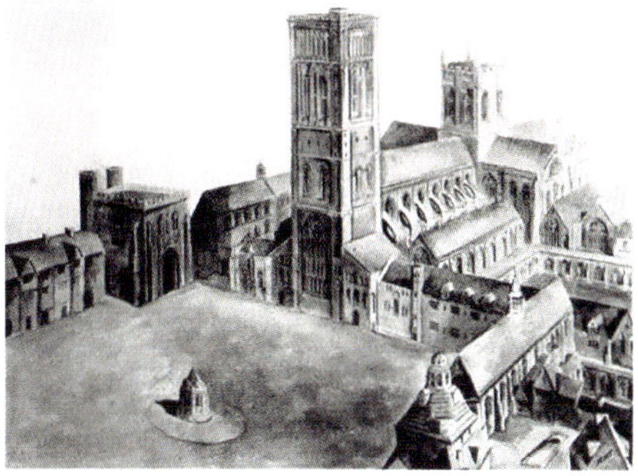

Picture of Oseney Abbey
Oxfordshire County Council photographic archive

of every persuasion, which set up schools to train their monks and established the precedent that religion and education were inseparable. That is why all scholars at Oxford were clerks in holy orders until as late as the nineteenth century, and most became priests.

The Priory of Saint Frideswide continued its existence at the centre of Oxford life for around 400 years but, as with many religious houses, it had its ups and downs. Its canons and clergy were not immune to temptations and bad behaviour, and many instances of wrongdoing were dealt with by charters now recorded in the Cartulary of St Frideswide, published in 1895 by the Oxford Historical Society. Some might say that the ruined abbeys of today are far more holy and peaceful than ever they were as functioning monasteries, and there are many charters still existing that suggest Saint Frideswide's was no exception.

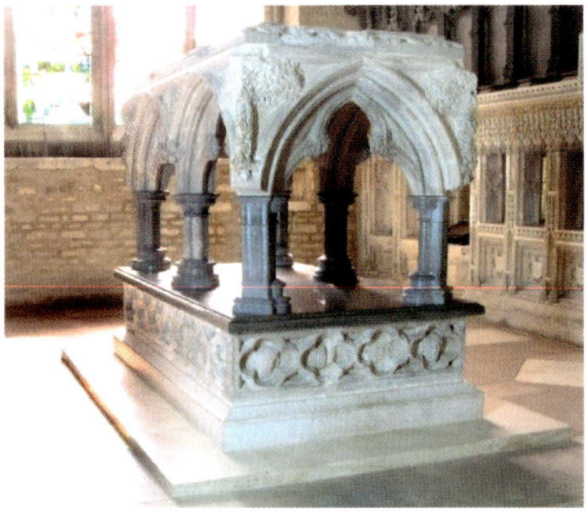

Reconstructed shrine in Latin chapel

However, the English Reformation resulted in a deliberate and devastating loss of the shrines and relics of saints, along with the irreplaceable destruction of the medieval art associated with them, and in this too Saint Frideswide's was no exception. In 1538, the cathedral was entered by the soldiers of Henry VIII, swords drawn, bent on destroying popish idolatry and adding valuable ecclesiastical treasures to the king's coffers.

The second, thirteenth-century, shrine of Saint Frideswide, dedicated on 10th September 1289, was desecrated in their greed. They took the jewels from her feretory (decorated coffin) and other valuable offerings for the king's treasury, leaving only her bones to be rescued by faithful men. They were eventually reburied in 1561 in the remains of her shrine. However, the seventeenth century reordering of the church under Dean Duppa (appointed 1629)[2] swept away the remains and covered up the original position of her shrine so that her final place of burial has been lost.

For around three hundred years, Frideswide, the Roman Catholic Patron Saint of the foremost university in the most prestigious city of England, was ignored in the zeal for Protestantism.

A Stained-Glass Virgin

The way Christ Church Cathedral reconnected with its saint started with a bequest by a Dr John Bull, a Canon of the Cathedral, who died in 1858. John Bull had first come up to Christ Church as a student in 1808.

He remained as a tutor and he was said to have *'the liveliest perception of the beauties of classical literature, as well as great power of communicating it to others'*.[3]

He was made a Canon in 1830 and was college Treasurer between 1832 and 1857, during which time he was said to have *'saved the college from ruin'* [4] with an astute financial decision. There is a monument to him high up on the western wall of the Latin Chapel opposite the beautiful window constructed as a result of his bequest.[5]

In his will he bequeathed £500 to the Dean and Chapter for two painted windows to replace the one at the east end of the Latin chapel, with the proviso that they were installed within three years.[6] Dean Henry Liddell (Dean 1855-92) had transferred the fourteenth century glass, which included the earliest known image of Saint Frideswide, into the side windows of the Latin chapel sometime after his installation in 1855.[7] It had managed to escape the destruction by Henry VIII's soldiers, being elsewhere in the Cathedral, and Mr Benjamin Woodward the Cathedral architect decided, possibly in discussion with the Dean, that the John Bull bequest should be used to fund a new stained-glass window of the St Frideswide legend, since her image already graced the Latin Chapel. [8]

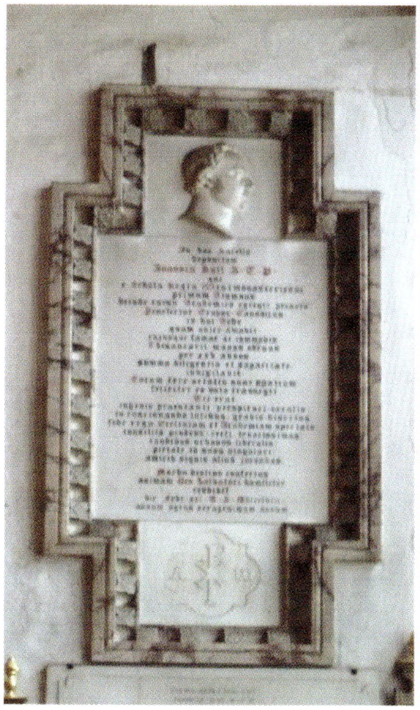

John Bull memorial in Latin chapel

In 1856, Ned Jones, a 23-year-old undergraduate of Exeter College, Oxford who had been impressed by the paintings of the Pre-Raphaelites and in particular Dante Gabriel Rossetti, approached Rossetti for tuition.[9] Jones had gone up to Oxford from Birmingham, funded by his father, planning to enter the church.[10] He met William Morris almost immediately[11] and both men became inspired by tales of high romance from medieval literature.[12] They also read lectures by Ruskin, the great nineteenth century art critic, and these made them aware of the controversial changes in art being pioneered by modern painters such as Rossetti.

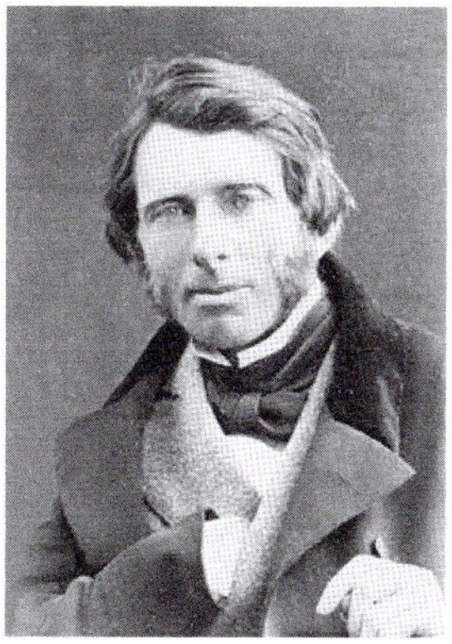

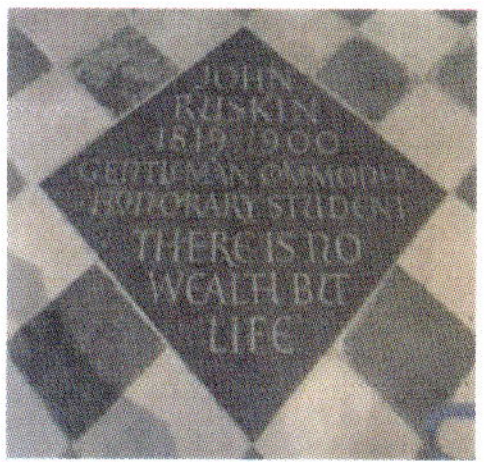

John Ruskin and his memorial

Ruskin felt the Pre-Raphaelites held the key to the development of *'truth and spirituality'* [13] in painting, and the reading of his lectures fired both men with a desire to see the paintings and meet the artists.[14] Morris and Jones were both unknown students at this point and could not just walk into the studios of great men, but when some Pre-Raphaelite paintings came to a Wyatt's gallery in the High Street in 1854, they were allowed to view them, on sufferance, by the owner.[15]

Millais's **Return of the Dove to the Arc** made a deep impression on Jones[16] and he was inspired to become a painter.[17] He left Oxford in 1856 almost penniless[18] and without a degree,[19] to train with Rossetti.[20] On seeing his developing talent, Rossetti insisted that he *'ought to be, and must be, an artist and so he became one'*. [21]

Towards the end of 1856 Morris joined Jones in London and they lived together at 17 Red Lion Square. Rossetti had lived there previously[22] and here Jones started painting in earnest.[23] He began to meet other artists, some of whom became life-long friends and would join him and Morris only a few years later in the firm of

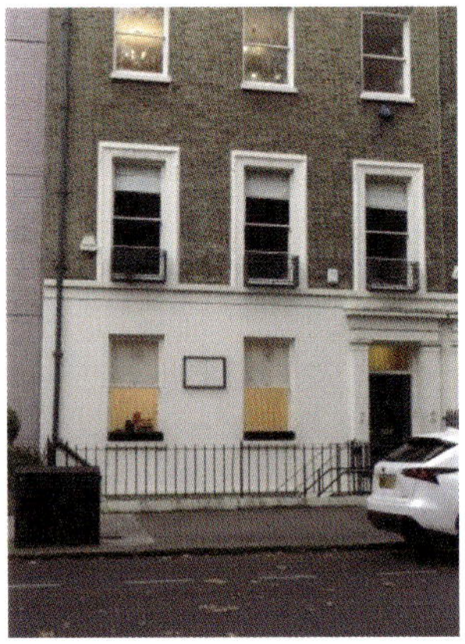

17 Red Lion Square, Holborn, London

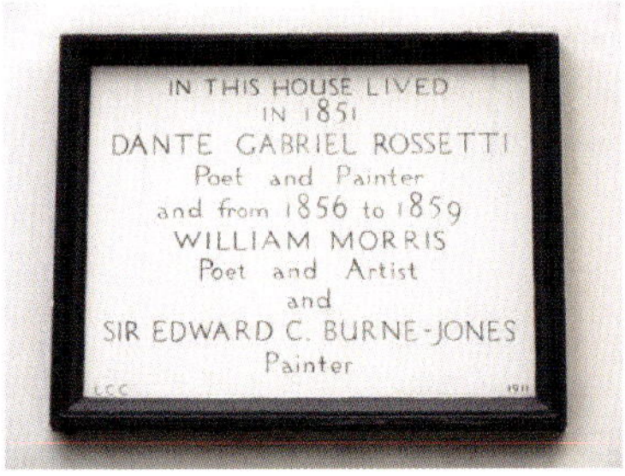

Plaque at 17 Red Lion Square

Morris and Co. Before 1856 had ended, Jones was introduced to John Ruskin who began to visit every week, encouraging and mentoring him as he worked out for himself how to be an artist.[24] His progress was remarkable.

In 1857, Rossetti introduced the 24-year-old[25] Jones to James Powell and Sons of the Whitechapel Glass Works, a firm of stained-glass manufacturers. According to May Morris much later, Rossetti told them that a *'young chap called Jones would do them some good stuff'* [26] and, according to the historian Percy Dearmer, they *'had the penetration to recognise his worth and employ him'*.[27] Jones designed two windows for Powell's during 1857.

Benjamin Woodward was the architect of the Oxford Museum and the Oxford Union buildings[28] and a friend of John Ruskin. He was also a friend of the Pre-Raphaelites, who Ruskin patronised, and knew Rossetti.[29] Woodward was looking for young artists to complete his Oxford building projects[30] with decorations and stained glass and was drawn to the new art movement. He probably got to know Jones through Rossetti in 1857 when he and his friends were decorating the Oxford Student Union Old Debating Hall and may have known Jones was working for Powell's.

Although Jones kept his lodgings in Red Lion Square, he and Morris had to take lodgings in Oxford during their time decorating the Student Union Hall. The first was in 87 High St, but they later moved to 13 George St, which was closer to the Student Union Buildings in St Michael's St. It was during this time that Morris met and fell in love with Jane Burden and, by February 1858, when most of the work was completed, Morris remained in Oxford to court her while Jones moved back to Red Lion Square.

When John Bull died in February 1858 and Benjamin Woodward was given the commission for the Frideswide window, he would have been aware of the work Jones had done on the walls of the Debating Hall and known that he was already designing windows for Powell's, so he approached James Powell and Sons with Jones in mind to do the design.[31] After he moved back to London, Jones fell seriously ill and had to be looked after by the mother of Val Prinsep, one of his friends. 1858 was the year of 'the great stink' in London and the excessive sewage which had been pumped into the Thames was causing serious health problems for many. Jones did not emerge from his sickness until September 1858 but may have been working on his commission from Powell's during this time or in the later part of the year.[32]

This series of events is pertinent when we see that Jones inserted a flush toilet into the last panel of the Frideswide window, her death bed scene. He wished no doubt for her to have the latest sanitary arrangements, and perhaps hoped that her untimely death was not as a result of lack of hygiene which had dispatched so many in London that year and may even had carried him off without the kindness of his friends who nursed him to health. The window was probably being installed in the cathedral at the end of 1858 or beginning of 1859 since it is known that Jones was in Oxford in March 1859 inspecting the finished job.[33]

During 1858 Jones was still very much learning his trade, but he was unable to continue living at Red Lion Square after September 1858 as Morris had decided to build his own home and had even bought land in Kent when he would soon commission his newly formed group of artistic friends to build and decorate his new home. He called it the Red House and it was his first married home, and the inspirational hub of his fledgling company Morris and Co. Jones moved on to 24 Russell Place, now renamed Fitzroy Street.[34]

The Frideswide window at Christ Church was only the fourth stained-glass window design Ned Jones had ever done. **His very first design in 1857** was for a single light in a window in **St Columba's church, Topcliffe, Yorkshire for the firm of Lavers and Barraud,** a stained-glass manufacturing business that had only been formed in 1855.[35] The window is on the south side of the chancel and his design for the Annunciation is the left light. Alongside it are the Visitation and the Nativity designed by Michael F. Halliday, a pupil of William Holman Hunt, and the Pre-Raphaelite influence is very strong in all three lights.[36]

This first window was the only window that shows his initials, apart from the Vyner window in the Lady Chapel at Christ Church Cathedral, Oxford. The design helpfully includes the words *Ave Maria dominus est tecum* (Hail Mary, the Lord is with you) to tell us what the window is about.

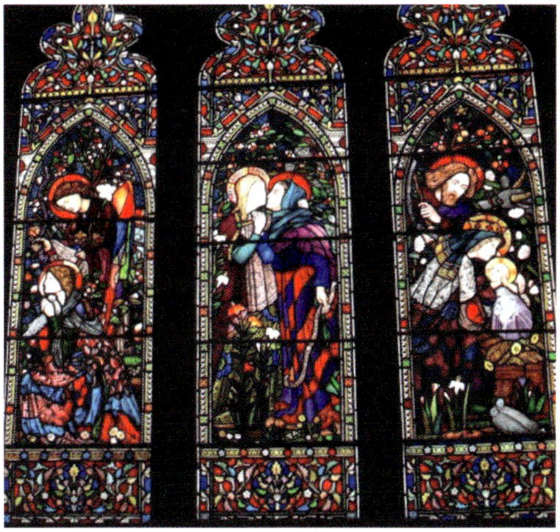

St Columba's church Topcliffe

The first window that Jones designed for James Powell and Sons, and his second overall, was the **Good Shepherd, 1857, for King Street United Reformed Church** (or Congregational Church as it was then known), at Maidstone in Kent.[37] The window is no longer in the church building, which has been decommissioned. It now resides as a stained-glass panel in Birmingham Art Gallery.

The usual practice was for the artist to prepare a cartoon (a representation) of the finished window which the stained-glass cutters could work from to create the window. Later cartoons were prepared as black and white line drawings but at this early stage, Jones was working in colour. A full colour cartoon of the Good Shepherd window is kept in storage at the Victoria and Albert Museum. A rare example of the creative genius of a young artist.

He depicts the shepherd as a large central figure in a pastoral setting holding a sheep on his shoulders and there are further sheep around his feet. It was placed in the church in 1861 and later received the acclaim that it showed a *'remarkable... understanding of two-dimensional design'* for an artist *'with no formal training or previous experience.'* [38]

Ruskin was *'impressed by the modesty and naturalism of the representation of Christ as a real shepherd'* in this window.[39] However, Jones' biographer Penelope Fitzgerald was less effusive in her description of it as *'a strong apprentice's design in Rossetti manner, a broad-hatted Christ with nail-holes in large square hands, "in such a dress as is fit for walking the fields and hills", carrying a sheep which chews the vine leaves around his hat.'* [40]

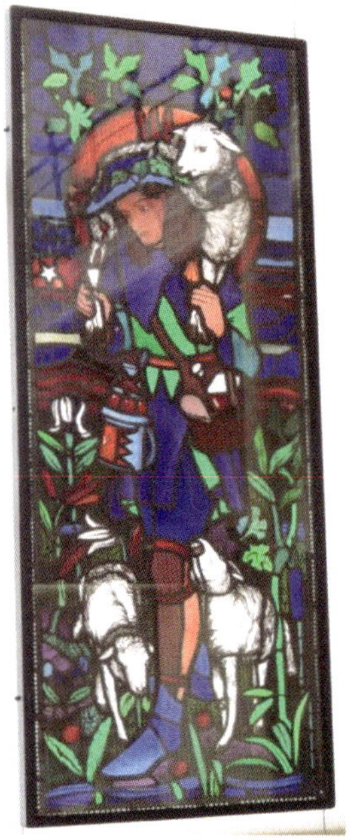

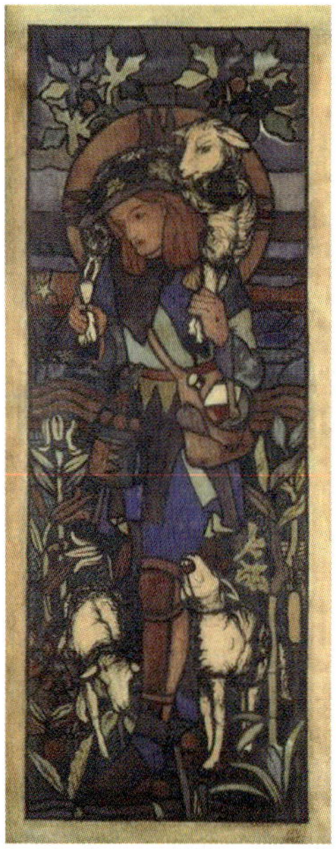

Good Shepherd window and cartoon

His second window for Powell's and third window in total, also designed in 1857 just before the Frideswide window, was **for the dining hall of St Andrew's College, Bradfield,** a public school, founded in 1850, by the Rev Stevens, the Rector of Bradfield.[41] In its architecture and decorations, the school has characteristics of the early Arts and Crafts movement. The window consisted of a triple-light of Adam and Eve, the Tower of Babel, and Solomon and Sheba, surmounted by *'a rose window of the seven Days of Creation.'* [42]

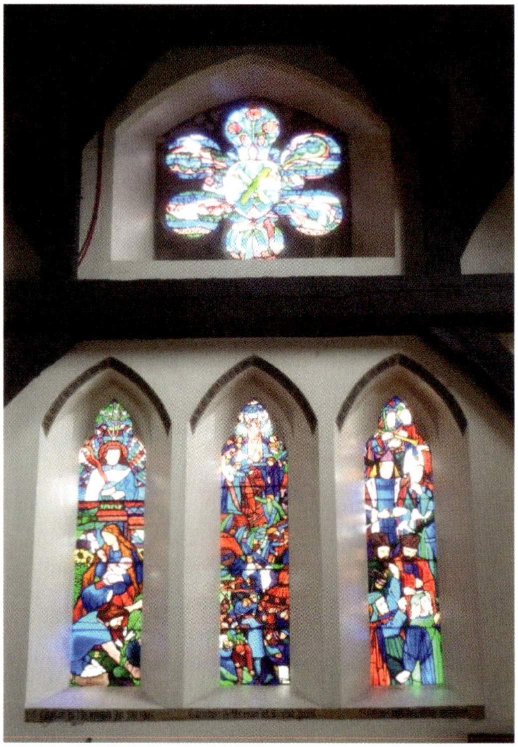

Bradfield College window

Each light of the window contains several scenes from the chosen Biblical story, indicated by figures performing tasks or striking poses. The figures are of differing sizes in the three lights and there is little to hold the scenes together or guide the eye throughout each light.

Although as brightly coloured as the Frideswide window and as attractive in presentation, it is difficult to decipher the meaning of the scenes. The rose window is, however, reminiscent of the six-petalled lights in the tracery of the Frideswide window.

How Jones became involved in this design is not exactly known. The dining hall was built in 1856 by the architect Sir George Gilbert Scott. In 1857 he commissioned Powell's to create the stained-glass window, and they must have engaged Jones, their new designer, to do his second design for them.

Gilbert Scott was the architect of Exeter College Library in 1857. He must have known that Rossetti was masterminding the re-decoration of the Old Debating Hall at the Oxford Union Society, for the architect Benjamin Woodward, along with his Pre-Raphaelite colleagues Val Prinsep, Spencer Stanhope and Algernon Swinburne. William Morris was also involved, as was Rossetti's new protégé Burne Jones, and John Ruskin was also *'instrumental in the work'*, his patronage of this new art movement being well known.[43]

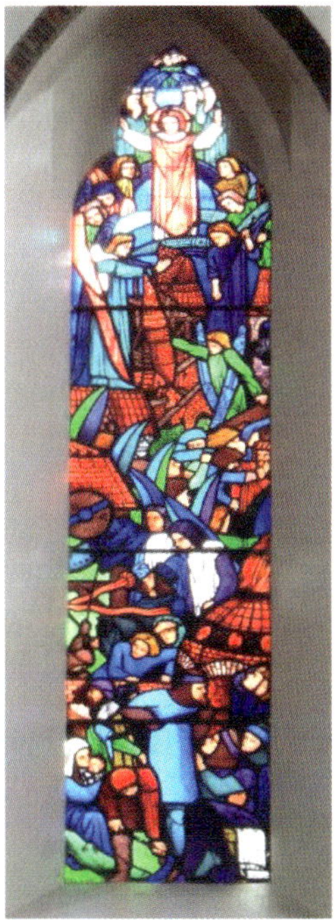

Central light – Tower of Babel

Gilbert Scott may well have been aware of Burne Jones and his association with Powell's through Rossetti or Ruskin and was willing to hazard his window design on a new artist in this new art movement if Powell's was willing to recommend him.

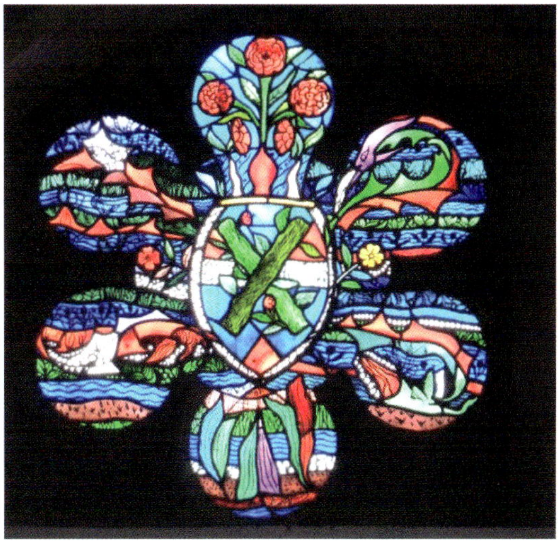

Rose window

There is also an outside chance that the first headmaster of the school, a Rev F B Guy 1850-1852, of Lincoln College, Oxford, had a hand in the choice. After he left Bradfield College, he went on to take William Morris as a private pupil[44] at Morris's home at Walthamstow in 1853,[45] before Morris went up to Oxford later that same year and may have kept in touch. If that was the case, he would have learnt about Burne Jones through Morris and recommended him to the Bradfield College founder, as able to achieve an appropriately modern design.

These three window designs, only a year or so after he had left Oxford, suggest that Jones, once he started painting, had an exceptionally rapid expansion of his talent.[46] These windows, and **a further window, his fifth, at Waltham Abbey in 1859,** are very different from his later work with the firm of Morris and Co. They all show strong Pre-Raphaelite influences,[47] and are full of complex detail, telling a developing story in each light.

The Frideswide window was his next and fourth commission. It is unknown what caused Benjamin Woodward and James Powell to be so confident that Jones could do so large and complex a work as the Frideswide window, telling a complete legend of a saint in stained glass so early in his career. His two completed Powell commissions had given him a strong foundation, but speculation would suggest that it was his patronage by Rossetti, who was a very respected figure, as well as a commendation by Ruskin, whose opinion was considered very highly by the art world that sealed the deal.

Rossetti informed Powell's that Ruskin was being *'driven wild with joy'* over Jones' early stained-glass designs, particularly that of the Good Shepherd,[48] but Rossetti had also been there when Ruskin had admired some of Jones' other drawings, and declared *'Jones, you are gigantic.'* [49]

Ned Jones was a rather small, slim person who liked to portray himself in cartoons as thin and weedy next to his rotund friend, William Morris, or Topsy as he was known to his friends. He was from then on referred to as *'gigantic Jones'* by the amused Rossetti.[50] These men had evidently spotted a unique talent at its early stages and were determined to encourage it.

The gamble Christ Church had taken in commissioning Jones, must have looked as though it had failed when the window was fitted. Many of its panels had half-cut figures at the edges and the scenes were crowded. It left the viewer looking at blobs and blotches of vivid colours, with little idea what they represented. One critic later referred to it dismissively, when viewed from a distance, as having *'a spotty kaleidoscopic effect which conveys no meaning to the eye.'* [51]

For a man of Ned Jones modest and melancholic character,[52] such early criticism might have finished his career forever, so it is fortuitous that the unflattering critiques were not published until after his death, when his reputation was unimpeachable.

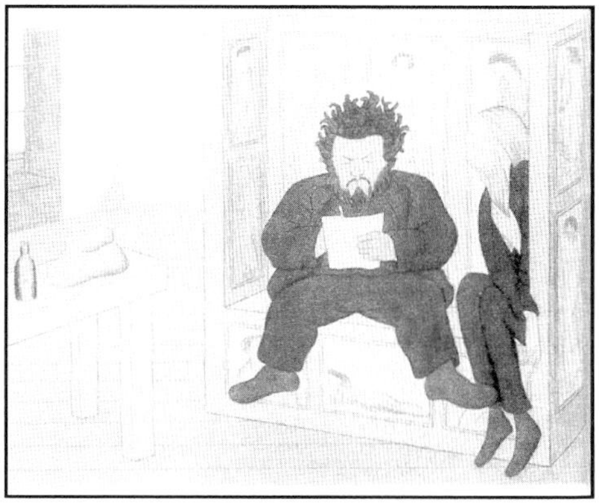

Cartoon by Jones of himself and Morris

The problem was one of inexperience by Jones, in putting too much detail into each panel, but it was compounded by an unfortunate mistake in measurements by the architect, Benjamin Woodward, who was seriously ill, and indeed died shortly afterwards.[53] As a result, the artist's design had to undergo a mechanical reduction by the stained-glass manufacturer before it could be fitted into the stone-mullioned window, making each scene more crowded than the artist intended. [54]

Looking at an old etching of the Latin Chapel before 1859, the stonework of the east window is in a simpler form, very different to the new tracery. It suggests that the whole stonework of the window must have been redesigned along with the new glass.

One source has described it as *'strangely incongruous Venetian tracery'*,[55] but a letter in the Christ Church archives written by Ned Jones himself gives us some light on the subject. *'...I have completed the cartoons and Powell will have them in hand at once. Also, I have written to Mr Bramwell to send me an exact cartoon of the head of the window, which I will design directly both with glass and carving.'* [56] It appears that Jones designed the tracery of the window himself and the ancient design he used, which was typical of his love of medievalism, filled with very modern stained glass must have seemed strange, and indeed incongruous, to the early viewers, though very beautiful today.

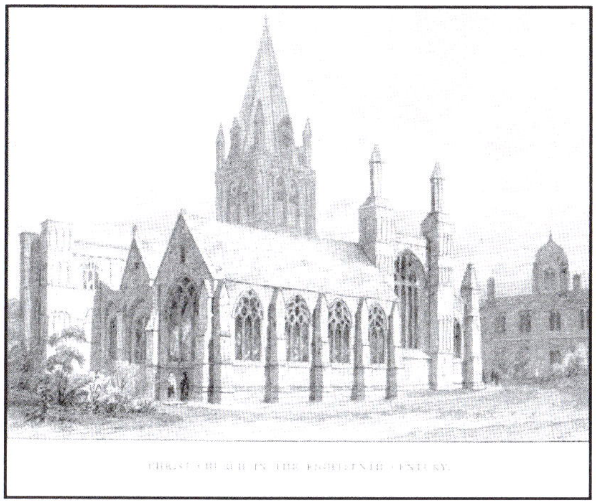

Etching of east end of Latin chapel

The designing of the stonework in which the glass would be inserted, seems to have been the normal practice for stained-glass artists in the early part of the nineteenth century. It was not until the formation of the firm of Morris and Co. in 1861, that architects began working closely with designers. Philip Webb,[57] an architect and one of the partners at Morris and Co., designed the architecture of many of the firm's early windows,[58] and this became a feature of the way Morris and Co. worked.

However, the Frideswide window was early in Ned Jones' career and one can only imagine his anxiety to get it right, and the heart-sink he felt when he saw the finished window. He had been paid £100 of the £500 it cost,[59] but it is said he was so dissatisfied with it that he *'offered to supply another window out of his own pocket.'* But the executors of Dr Bull's will, after some deliberation, said *'they were content with the end product and refused to countenance any change'*.[60]

Fortunately, it did not put Ned off designing stained glass, as two of his further windows have similar detailed work. The first of these, **his fifth window, was the Jesse Tree windows at Holy Cross and St Lawrence Church, Waltham Abbey,**[61] designed in 1859[62] before he joined Morris and Co. but fitted in 1860-61.[63]

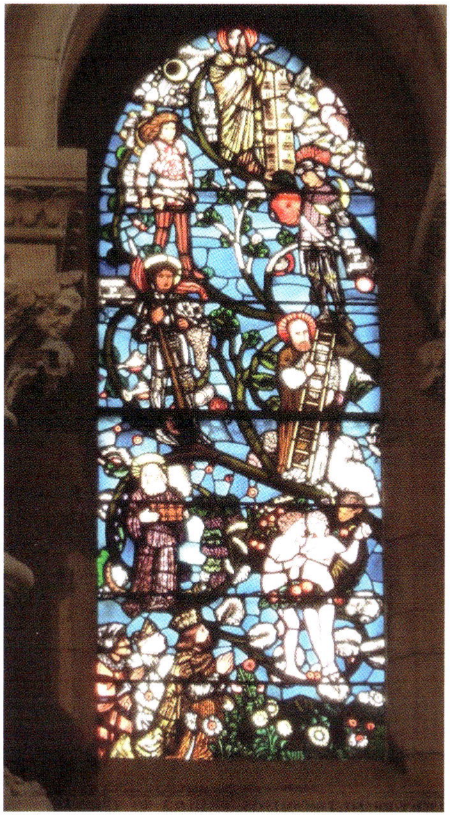

Waltham Abbey window left light

The three lights of the windows high up at the east end of the church are filled with figures from the Bible helpfully linked by the trunk and branches of the Jesse Tree. With closer inspection the figures also have labels to indicate who they are. The linkage and labels show a development in his sense of design and Ned must have either realised or been told that he needed to be do something to help his viewers understand the scenes.

The second of the two further windows, **his sixth altogether, is the four-light window of 1863 in the south transept at St Michael's and All Angels church, Lyndhurst, Hants,** depicting Joshua, Elijah, St Stephen and St Peter.[64] Again it is over-loaded with *'pictorial incident'* in a similar way to the Frideswide window at Christ Church and the Bradfield College windows.[65]

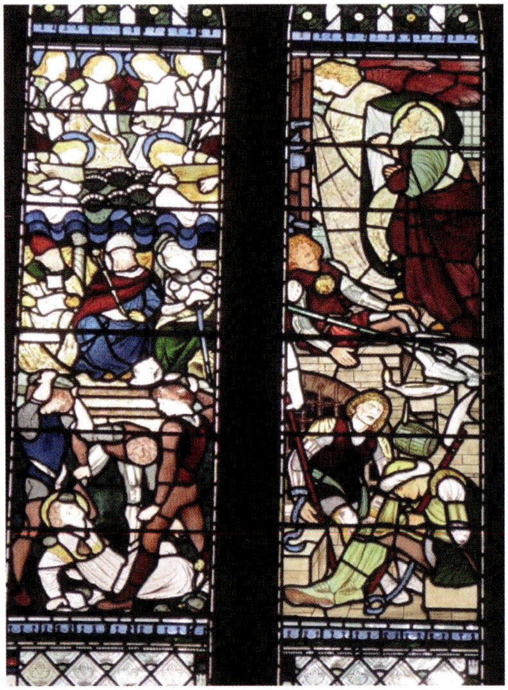

Two panels of the Lyndhurst window

The criticism has been made that these early windows are confusing to an untrained eye especially when viewed from a distance, and it is a valid criticism. However, when each of these windows is carefully viewed from close up, it can be seen that they have been *'composed with consummate mastery'*.[66] This design style was a short-lived phase in the very early career of Ned Jones when he was struggling to find his genre, and these six windows are the only major works by him in this same style.

The Waltham Abbey window was designed directly for Powell's as part of an 1859/60 restoration of the church, but the later window at Lyndhurst was made by Morris and Co. By then William Morris was personally overseeing all the designs and reviewed the finished effect. It is evident that he recognised the mistake Jones was making as *'no other window by the firm errs in this way'*.[67] Indeed, Morris co-designed many windows himself and he probably guided Jones towards his later style, where the scenes were clearer and the figures more prominent.

This is shown in **his seventh window, the Song of Solomon window in St Helen's Church, Darley Dale, Derbyshire, by Morris and Co. 1862-63.**[68] It is a complex story like Saint Frideswide, but he has taken a step forward in his composition. The figures are more distinct, and the scenes are depicted in separate panels.

However, in this case the separations between the panels are strong and the same in all three lights. There are even a couple of lines of narrative beneath each panel, so the viewer has no excuse not to understand the meaning. In this we can see that his partnership with Morris was setting Jones well on the way to becoming the famous creator of so many stunning, individual, stained-glass windows with figures that are as clear as they are beautiful.

Edward Burne Jones designed several other windows in Christ Church Cathedral Oxford, including Faith, Hope and Charity 1871, in the west end of the South aisle; the Vyner Memorial Window 1872, in the Lady Chapel; the St Cecilia Window 1874, in the Bell Chapel; and the 1878 St Catherine Window in the Regimental Chapel. They were done when he was at the height of his powers as an artist and are quite different in style and pictorial representation from the St

Frideswide window. I wonder how his mature self viewed his early attempt at telling a story in stained glass? [69]

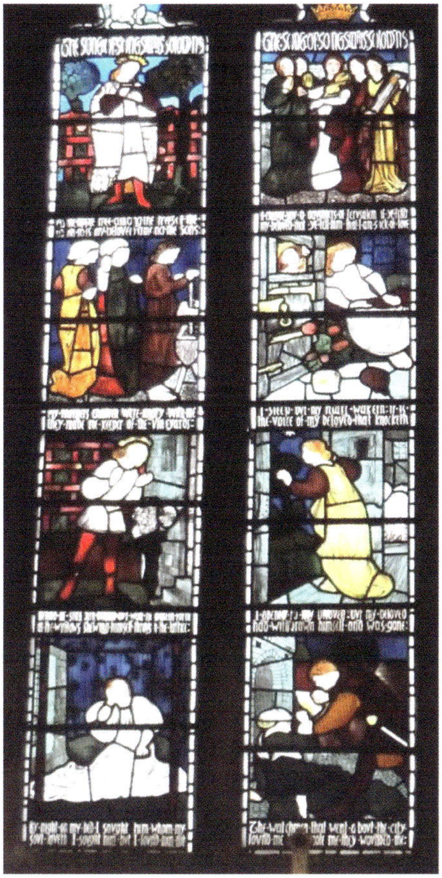

Two panels of St Helen Darley Dale

However, tucked away in a quiet part of Christ Church Cathedral is one window in a similar style to Jones' Bradfield College and Waltham Abbey windows. It is by a different artist and shows that he was not alone in his struggle to tell a story in stained glass. It is a round-headed window set into one of the restored Norman windows of the church, and it is just to the left of the door into the cloister from the south aisle of the nave.

It is the Life of St Peter by James E Rogers, manufactured by James Powell and Sons in 1864 and is therefore closer to the time of the Frideswide window than any of the other pre-Raphaelite windows in the cathedral. It tells the story of St Peter, and the scenes travel from the bottom to the top. It starts with his calling by Jesus when a humble fisherman, *'I will make you fishers of men'* at the bottom, through walking on the water *'O ye of little faith'*, to his escape from prison and from death with the help of an angel at the top.

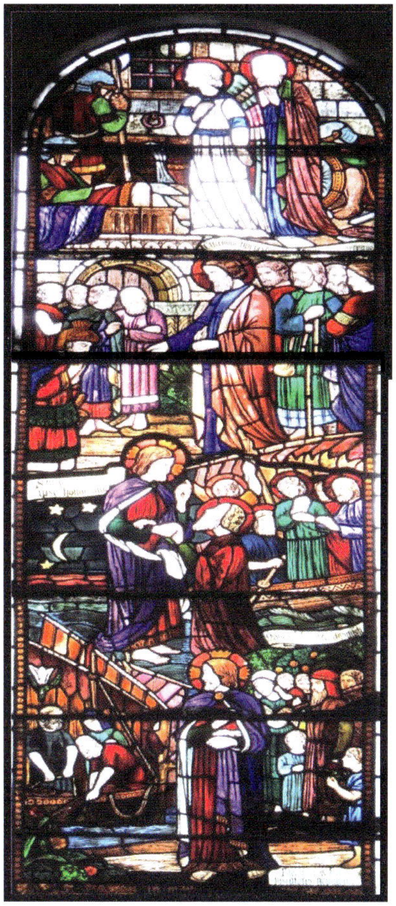

South nave aisle window

The four scenes have strong Pre-Raphaelite influences and slightly overlap one another with only the design thread of similarity in content and colour to hold them together. Scrolls of Latin text illuminate the content, but they are only helpful so long as the viewer is familiar with Latin.

None of these six early works of Burne Jones, not even the Frideswide Window, are mentioned in any detail in his biographies. In books of Pre-Raphaelite art, they are either not there at all, or glossed over with barely a paragraph. It is almost as if they and, for our interest the Frideswide window, have been airbrushed from his compendium of works, as though publishers dismiss them as the juvenile work of a young artist: not very good and best forgotten.

Yet these windows show a clear development in his work as a stained-glass designer and are worthy of study in their own right. They have greater depth than many of his later works and draw you in to examine the subject depicted. Indeed, when viewed closely, as one critic enthuses, the Frideswide window at least *'carries on the best traditions of the craft, in its infinite variety of gem-like colours and complexity of detail.'* [70] It also *'attains a degree of perfection in its pictorial effect and figure drawing which was impossible during earlier eras of medieval glass painting'*.[71] Another critic describes it as *'evoking the spirit of medieval glass without directly imitating its form.'* [72]

However, the Frideswide window has one problem that the others do not suffer from and that is the difficulty of viewing the window. From the best of intentions, the newly re-constructed shrine of St Frideswide was placed just in front of it in 2002. Although the glowing colour of the Frideswide window gives the shrine a stunning backdrop, it heightens the problems of the window design.[73]

The Latin Chapel was chosen for the shrine because it was thought by historians to be closest to where the original grave of Saint Frideswide may have been situated, in her early monastery church, though this is debated. It was also close to the fourteenth-century window of the saint in the north wall of the chapel, and near the fifteenth century 'watching chamber', which contains a chantry chapel and may have been used to watch over the valuable second shrine originally situated in the near-by Lady Chapel.

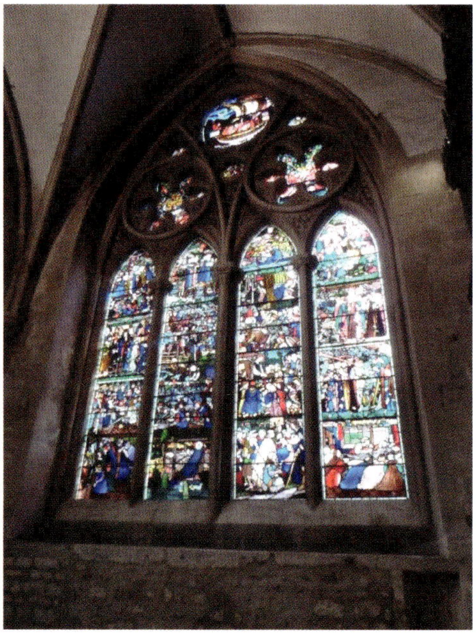

Frideswide window from close beneath

However appropriate or not the chosen position for the shrine may be, the unfortunate result is a narrowing of the space available for people to get a proper look at the window. The visitors must either stand just beneath and crane their necks to look up, or stand beyond the shrine, and use binoculars or risk eyestrain, in their efforts to make out the panels from a distance. The comments of visitors trying to understand the window, and the way in which they turn from it after looking only at the lowest panels, bears out the problems of its present arrangement.

However, many problems can be resolved with enough time, and as one critic says, *'When one has sat down for five to ten minutes and deciphered the various scenes, its unapproachable beauty becomes apparent, and each succeeding visit deepens the impression of the splendour and poetry of this incomparable work.'* [74]

Another critic agrees that *'From a distance it gives an overall impression of deep brilliant colour,'* but *'as one draws closer, each scene and figure fits into place, forming a very dense mass of narrative detail.'* [75] He considered that the Frideswide window was *'the finest of the early works'* [76] of Sir Edward Burne-Jones.

Creating a Masterpiece

When you look at the lasting brilliance of the colours of the stained glass in the Frideswide window it is noticeably different from other windows nearby in the Cathedral, even from windows as close to it in time as the 1840s. This is because Powell's had been looking for new technology to improve the colours, and they welcomed the research of a barrister called Charles Winston.[77]

In 1849,[78] Winston had sent pieces of medieval glass for chemical analysis to a Dr Medlock of the Royal College of Chemistry,[79] in the hope of discovering how it was made and analysing the colours. Powell's was the first stained-glass manufacturer to use these results to make their 'new' glass[80] and, by 1856,[81] Powell's had succeeded in making a beautifully streaky 'flashed' ruby glass (a clear glass coated with a thin layer of red glass[82]) which can be seen in the Ship of Souls in the large round window of the upper tracery.[83]

They had also made a blue, a yellow, a white, several shades of green and some shades of purple.[84] The Frideswide window is the earliest place in which this new technology was used and the overall effect of the *'pure colour and brilliant tone'* [85] of the new glass has been described by some critics as a *'gorgeous mosaic of colour'* [86] or *'glowing with a kaleidoscopic range of colours.'* [87] As a pre-Morris design *'it is bolder and more forceful than Morris ever was'* [88] and in colour, even *'violent'* [89] with its preponderance of red,[90] but it is *'straight from Rossetti'* [91] in the types and style of the figures, showing how much Jones early friendship with Rossetti influenced his art. One critic adds that *'despite the medieval setting, Burne Jones' figures are not drawn in the stylised Gothic idiom favoured by Pugin and his followers, they are in pose and expression, as naturalistically conceived as the characters of a Pre-Raphaelite painting, with the same sense of dramatic intensity.'* [92]

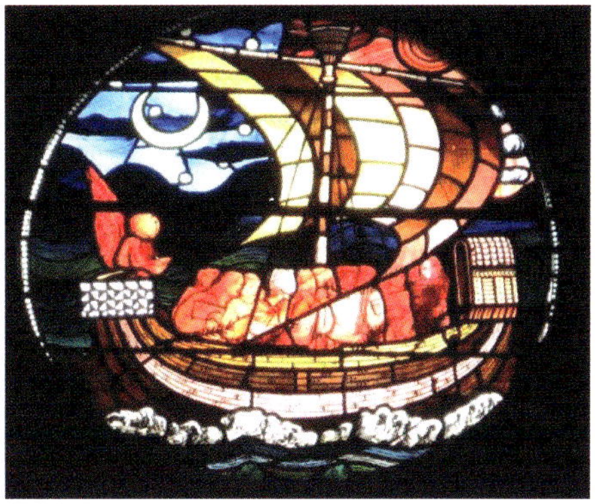

Ship of Souls roundel

An example of Rosetti's stained-glass work is in the east window of St Martin-on-the-Hill in Scarborough from 1862 (discussed on p52), which has such a remarkable resemblance to the 1858 Frideswide window that one might argue that Burne Jones was leading Rosetti in this aspect of his art.

It was also notable that Charles Winston advocated a new style of construction of the stained-glass windows, different from the styles in use at the time. This *'medieval method'* was rather like a mosaic. In a floor mosaic the design is built up with small pieces of coloured stones held together by cement, so Winston advocated that each brightly coloured piece of window glass be held together by strips of lead.[93] This *'ran counter to the eighteenth and early nineteenth century practice of painting figures on large pieces of clear glass.'* [94] Window artists from the eighteenth century had *'tended to think of stained glass simply as painting on a transparent material instead of canvas.'* [95] They relied to a great extent on *'copying paintings by old masters that had been intended for totally different purposes,'* [96] and it is thought by some critics that *'the resulting effect was somewhat unreal.'* [97]

Winston passionately believed in this alternative medieval mosaic method,[98] which was practiced in the first half of the sixteenth century in the Low Countries.[99] He called it the 'mosaic enamel method' and it *'employed both white and coloured glass in every known variety of stain and enamel colour.'* [100] He was however *'emphatic that mere imitation of the style and drawing of an earlier period should not be encouraged'* but felt that the *'charm of medieval work was due to the real artistic feeling and thorough conception of the subject which are expressed in it.'* [101] He wrote that *'for such qualities to be recovered, and for the advancement of stained-glass painting as an art, it was essential that* ***artists*** *be encouraged to practise it, in distinction to mere* ***artisans*** *who at present make it their trade.'* [102]

However, in 1857 there were few British glass-painter artists that Winston could recommend,[103] and many of them were still imitating historic styles.[104] They almost all fell short in *'creating major figure compositions with the expressive power of a great original piece of art'*.[105] Even Ned Jones, so early in his career, had not developed his distinct and individual style of major figure compositions in his stained-glass work, which was to later earn him a knighthood. A contributor to the Art Journal reviewing the stained-glass exhibits in the 1862 Exhibition, complained that *'it is the great error of our own best glass painters that they have been content to aim at reproducing old work... This copying... must give way to originality.'* [106]

The importance of Winston's work *'can hardly be exaggerated as the mosaic system became almost universally used, and within a few years supplanted the style of pictorial transparencies.'* [107] During Ned Jones' short contact with Powell's, before he joined Morris and Co. (who would soon manufacture their designs in their own studio [108] using glass supplied by Powell's[109]), he was drawn into using this new method,[110] building up his early designs by *'fitting individual colours together on the old lines'* to make the picture.[111] His method is confirmed by another source which agrees that *'in these first designs, he indicated the lead lines and the colouring himself',*[112] and some of his early cartoons (drawings or paintings on paper of his designs for the glass cutters to reproduce) show the lead lines clearly marked.[113]

The usual practice of stained-glass designers was to make a full-size painting, or pencil drawing which the glass manufacturers could use as a pattern when cutting and painting the final window. These were called cartoons and many of Burne Jones' cartoons survive in art galleries and museums across the country. Jones' early cartoons, painted in full colour for these, his first stained-glass windows, are works of art in themselves.

William Burges, an architect, wrote about the Frideswide window in the Gentlemen's Magazine of 1862 saying, *'Mr Jones is a colourist, and consequently declines to trust the choice of tones of his colours to the glass painter, he therefore makes a finished colour painting in oil, the result is that the best modern stained-glass windows are due to his design.'* [114]

However, this was short lived and, after he joined Morris and Co., he began to leave the choice of colour to others. Indeed, the art critic Christopher Wood disagreed with the Gentlemen's Magazine and felt that choice of colour was not one of Jones' strongest points. He states that *'Such distinctions that Burne Jones' early cartoons possessed was not significantly due to their colour; in a sense he was never much of a colourist, and consequently the greatest limitations of the work which Powell's did from his designs were due to their reliance on him at his weakest point.'* This was a real set-down and may simply be because the darkened varnish had altered the colours of the cartoons, as we shall see later, by the time of Christopher Wood's biography. However, it also shows how well Morris and Co. acted as a team, each working to his strengths.

All Jones' early windows have the same 'mosaic' lead work, with similar figures and storytelling, but his style was maturing rapidly. The first windows made in the studio of Morris and Co. after it was formed in 1861 were not designed exclusively by him. The firm started by using several artists to design and work on each window and initially they used the paler, older style[115] of stained glass, that *'produced very little impact.'* [116]

They soon changed to the new glass, and commissions began to arrive for large windows with complex designs that required a range of skills. Christopher Wood, in his book, Burne-Jones, tells us that *'To begin, the success of Morris and Co. was entirely due to their stained glass'*, because *'In the 1860s they received a number of important commissions, mainly due to Morris and Webb's contact with many of the leading architects of the day.'* [117]

In these early years Burne Jones worked alongside William Morris, Philip Webb, Ford Madox Brown, and others in producing each window.[118] Morris, and there was no disagreement among critics about this, was *'primarily a colourist and decorator'*, but was also good at seeing the bigger picture of the window design within the framework of a building and at choosing the colours.[119] Webb, the architect, would plan the layout of the window and produce scale drawings with all the architectural details.[120] Madox Brown was a figure painter, like Burne Jones, but he loved invention, expression and action. [121] Jones became supreme at static figures with multiple folds of drapery as well as filling the space with foliage and other detail.

The outstanding fact about the stained glass produced in the Morris studio was that *'imaginative'* designs were combined with *'remarkable decorative craftsmanship'* and *'colouristic genius, which meant they were not easily surpassed in quality and originality.'* [122] However, Charles Winston's mosaic system was only used for a limited period as it produced a rather bitty and confused appearance in the windows, and his influence seems to be the source of the drawbacks and problems in Burne Jones' design of the Frideswide window.

As the recognisable Burne Jones style developed with phenomenal speed, his mature designs had fewer lead lines and were less fussy in detail. He returned to painting onto the glass and began to concentrate on beautifully defined individual figures with flowing robes, the over-riding style that dominated the later part of his career.

Burne Jones and the Art World

The partnership between Burne Jones and William Morris occurred at a perfect moment of transition in the world of art, and that is why it was so successful. The early nineteenth century Gothic revival, which reached its peak in the mid-nineteenth century, was beginning to lose its popularity and the art world was ready for new styles and designs.[123] Even though the new themes were a return to medievalism, the clarity and simplicity of the designs, built on the Pre-Raphaelite model, were new and exciting.

The art world was slow to catch on to the genius of this new group of designers, but their stained-glass windows carried them along in the early years when their paintings were shunned or criticised by the Royal Academy. It was the nineteenth-century revival in religious observance that made stained glass so popular, especially the increase in church attendance which led to a boom in the building of new churches and the restoration of old ones. Whether new or old, the large, east-end windows in these churches needed beautiful glass decorations, and there were many more windows in the naves and aisles. The developing fashion for memorial windows[124] fitted this niche perfectly, and they were privately funded by the increasingly prosperous middle classes who, along with everyone else, were affected by the high death rates.

It also helped the new designers that during the first quarter of the nineteenth century a great deal of the stained glass was, as one critic has said, *'artistically negligible or deplorable, produced by artisans in commercial workshops simply as an article of trade, and as devoid of good drawing, imaginative design and profound feeling as of true understanding of the materials.'* [125]

Before the arrival of the Pre-Raphaelites, and Burne Jones in particular, the design of stained glass had been dominated by Pugin and was Gothic in style. Though Winston, who researched the new glass for Powell's, was a Renaissance man, he was an isolated figure among his contemporaries[126] and Gothic continued to remain influential until the 1870s with many of the glassmaking firms.

Plain Ned Jones challenged the pre-eminence of this style[127] with his early work, and for this alone the Frideswide window in Christ Church Cathedral is worthy of study. As one critic has said, *'Before the foundation of the Morris firm his work had advanced English stained glass from imitative medievalism to a modern creative art far ahead of anything being produced elsewhere.'* [128] It was a new beginning, a turning point, even a pivot on which a new depiction of the art of stained glass would revolve, and as such it is incomparable and *'a true masterpiece of Victorian stained glass'.*[129] Some critics even award him the honour of *'rejuvenating the tradition of stained-glass art in England',* [130] and an early commendation from 1862 states *'The window may be said to mark a decided step in the art of modern glass-staining.'* [131]

The Frideswide window at Oxford, the Jesse Tree windows at Waltham Abbey, and the later south aisle window at Lyndhurst, all show how Burne Jones had a *'capacity for large-scale decorative pattern which was quite unrivalled then and throughout his life'.*[132]

The ability of the firm to reproduce his designs for many different customers meant that his later stained-glass windows were installed in churches and important buildings throughout the length and breadth of the country, but despite his pre-eminence in the field he remained a modest and humble person. **However, his first six stained-glass creations were, and will always be, unique.** Their complexity and intensity ensured that they were never reproduced, and they will always remain a testament to a developing genius.

It was not until he was almost 50 that Burne Jones received the first of what became a series of awards, including an Honorary Degree at Oxford in 1881, although he had never completed his first degree. The culmination was a knighthood in 1894, when he was 61.

He legally hyphenated the Burne Jones name into Burne-Jones in February 1894, and in May 1894 he accepted the title of Sir Edward Coley Burne-Jones of Rottingdean, in the county of Sussex, and of the Grange, in the parish of Fulham, London.[133]

This was much to the chagrin of his wife, Georgina, who espoused the anti-establishment attitude of the pre-Raphaelite artists more than the artists themselves.

These vital young men, who pushed the boundaries of art in their youth, were gradually being sucked into the mainstream. Rossetti himself remained aloof, but Millais had accepted the presidency of the Royal Academy some time before. For Georgina, her husband's title was a step too far from their early ideals.

Sir Edward Coley Burne-Jones died in 1898, but his work was beginning not to sell by 1895,[134] and by the early twentieth century he was hopelessly out-of-fashion in the art world. It was only later in the twentieth and in the early twenty-first century that the skill and realism of the Pre-Raphaelite painters has been re-assessed and acclaimed.[135]

Sadly, the exhibition in 1933 at the Tate Gallery that marked the centenary of his birth was poorly attended and received unflattering reviews. However, the exhibition in 1998 that marked the 100th anniversary of his death, opened in the Metropolitan Museum of Art in New York to a quite different reception, before moving to the Birmingham Museum and Art Gallery, and the Musée d'Orsay in Paris.[136]

Prime Minister Stanley Baldwin, nephew of Burne-Jones, officially opened the 1933 exhibition and gave him this tribute... *'what he did for us common people was to open... magic casements of a land of faery in which he lived throughout his life... It is in that inner world that we can cherish, in peace and beauty, what he has left us... His work will be there forever for those who seek beauty and who can reverence a great man and a great artist.'* [137]

A more recent tribute from Christopher Wood in the foreword to the 2003 edition of the Burne-Jones biography by Penelope Fitzgerald is worth quoting. Wood, himself an author of a biography on Burne Jones and Pre-Raphaelitism, says that he (Burne-Jones) was *'an arch-dreamer and romantic'* fascinated by beauty. *'...he wanted as a young man to go into the church and when he decided to become an artist, he brought a sense of missionary fervour to his art. He transmuted his religious ideals into artistic ones... for him art had a duty to improve the world and to make it a better place.'* [138]

No wonder so much of his stained-glass work was centred around saints and angels. The legend of Saint Frideswide was his first, and most notable, representation of a non-biblical saint in stained glass.

Telling a Story in Glass

Technicalities

Using stained glass as a medium for storytelling is a unique form of art, quite different from painting on canvas, and poses interesting problems for an artist. What the artist has to work out, is how to tell a story that has movement in a medium that is static, and it is not an easy problem to solve. As one source has said *'It may be doubted whether stained glass lends itself very readily to narrative treatment.'* [139]

This was especially true of the Pre-Raphaelite painters, who Jones was emulating early in his career. Many of their paintings were inspired by legendary figures and literary heroes and they mostly dealt with the problem by depicting a snapshot from the narrative, with carefully posed and static figures.

Ned Jones was to pursue this method to perfection on canvas later in his career, but in the late 1850s, he was still discovering his talent and developing his craft. He was learning as he went along, and it was a remarkably steep learning curve. In his design for the Frideswide window, and his other early works, we are fortunate to be able to see some of this process.

Of course, the most important element of a stained-glass window design was what the client wanted, and it is possible that Jones had personal discussions with his client, the architect Benjamin Woodward, on site before he started work. He would need this to understand the size of the window and the dimensions of the space it illuminated. This would help him with the layout and colouring of the design. The usual practice was for the client to call at the manufacturer's premises later to discuss finer points and make further decisions if they so wished.[140]

In the 1850s, it was normal practice for the designer to draw a life-size coloured, or black-and-white cartoon[141] of his design for the glass-craftsman to make up, but a lot of things had to be taken into consideration first. Glass was a different medium from that to which most artists were accustomed, and the purpose of the window, and the way it would be viewed were totally different from a painting on canvas.[142]

A window would be looked at from a distance by an untrained, but spiritually aware audience, viewed against a background of daylight. This meant that the design needed to be clear and simple, with outlines more like a drawing than a painting.[143] Instead of the intricate detail and subtle variations of colours that enhance a painting on canvas, a design on glass needed cleaner lines and distinct colours. As we have seen, Ned Jones took some time to change his style from painting on canvas to drawing on the sky and needed some help to do so.[144] William Morris himself said in a pamphlet written for an art fair in 1883, that the discovery of how to do this effectively was *'an art apart.'* [145]

The context and position of the window within the church also needed to be considered. The light and clarity of the sun on the windows of the south side of a church would require different types of colours and textures from those on the darker, shadier north side.[146] Perhaps a dark chancel, or side chapel would need to be lightened up with pale glass, rather than be made even darker by deep colours.[147]

To be truly successful, a stained-glass window also needed to be pleasing to the eye, and this is best achieved by designing the window as a whole with similarity in the colour and scale of the design across all the lights of the window.[148] Ned Jones did not get this quite right in his Bradfield College design of 1857 (see p39), and one source describes it as exhibiting *'some odd disparities of scale between the three lights.'* [149]

The design would also need clear separations between distinct parts, preferably with the separating lines running across the

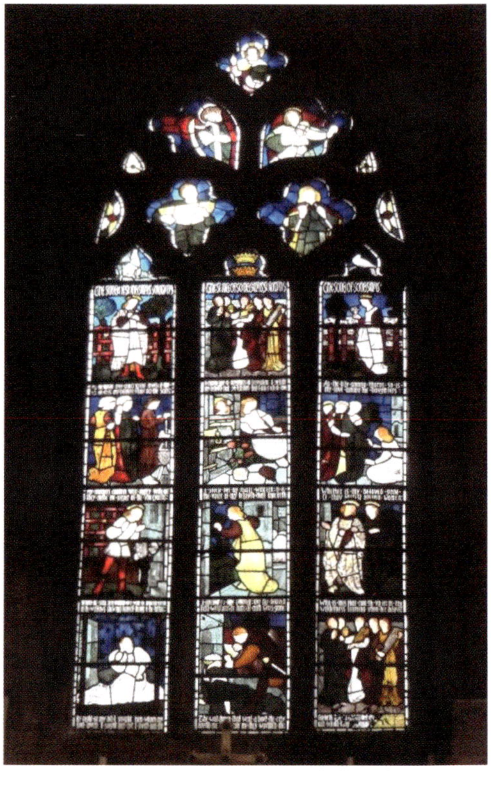

Darley Dale Song of Solomon window

whole window, so that each light had similar sizes of panels. This is particularly a problem with his sixth window, the Lyndhurst design of

1863 (see p42), where a critic comments that *'the way each light is treated independently from its neighbours'* with *'a lack of a horizontal relationship'* between them *'proves disturbing,'* [150] and this is one of the main reasons the window was less successful than it might have been. He did not do too badly in his Frideswide window, and he certainly managed to get it right in his seventh design, the Song of Solomon window at St Helen's Church, Darley Dale in Derbyshire.[151]

The separate lights of a large window were also generally very tall and thin, so attempting to depict the image or narrative within the space needed careful thought.[152] Should the principal scene be high or low in the space? What device could be used to tie together the different levels of the design? In his Jesse Tree design at Waltham Abbey, Jones solved this problem with the effective use of the trunk and branches of a tree, and James E Rogers used a curved line and Latin text in his window in the south nave aisle of Christ Church Cathedral.

The problem was that large figures filling the space higher up could feel top-heavy, but smaller figures lower down could feel 'bitty'.[153] It also meant that some sort of pattern, such a leaves or diamonds, would be needed to fill the empty sections of the design, risking making it too busy.[154]

The artist really needed to think of the window as a whole with the stonework and tracery, and the ideal was for the lower design to lead the eye up to something magnificent in the upper tracery, such as a rose window with Christ in Glory as in the nineteenth-century east window at Christ Church Cathedral Oxford, or the Ship of Souls in the Frideswide window, only yards away in the Latin Chapel.

As we have seen for the Frideswide window, Jones did all the design himself, [155] and this had been fairly normal up until the 1850s, before the advent of Morris and Co. The artist would deal directly with the glass manufacturer without the benefit of an overall designer to consider all the implications of the window project. Indeed, *'the unification of the process of design and execution in the person of one artist-craftsman'* became the Arts and Crafts Movement ideal.[156]

However, Morris soon began to realise that the artist and craftsman had quite different strengths, and very rarely were they both equally present in one person.[157] In his later partnership with Burne Jones, Morris was able to take the wider overview of each project to make sure that everything about the window, from the stonework to the coloured design, was harmonious within its setting.[158]

A few years later, Morris would learn that the technique and craft of making up the designs into glass also needed to be understood by the artist, to enable him to produce a technically feasible design. This was shown very clearly in an early window by Morris when a design by Rossetti was used for the east window of St Martin-on-the-Hill Church, Scarborough in 1862 (see page 52). [159] It consists of three lights surmounted by a rose window. In the centre light is a portrayal of the crucifixion by Ford Madox Brown surrounded by seven panels by Rossetti depicting the parable of the vineyard. These are very similar in style to the Frideswide window panels, full of colours and shapes that appear a confusing mosaic from the distance.

The problem was compounded when some of the shapes within the design were *'almost impossible to cut by the glassmaker'.* [160] It showed a lack of understanding of how glass breaks when scored and it was particularly true of Rossetti's panels. It needed the artists to *'watch the process of work in the glass studio and discuss any difficulty that arose in the course of the production.'* [161] Morris realised that this was essential in understanding *'the limitations and possibilities of stained glass'* [162] so that an effective design could be made.

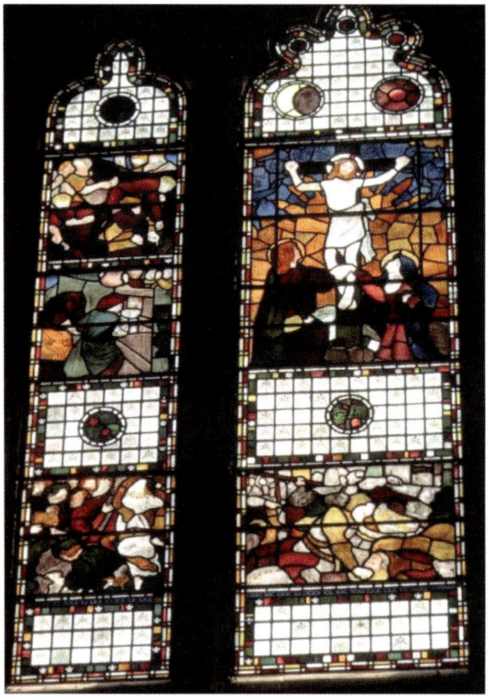

Scarborough window - left and central lights

Morris felt *'it was vitally important that the craftsmen of the studio, from himself down to the humblest cutter and glazier, should carry out their work with full professional efficiency,'* [163] and he believed that, if they worked together, they could produce an unrivalled product.[164] That is why so many of his early windows were designed by the partners as a team. Indeed, one critic has said that the *'outstanding fact about Morris's glass was that it was a product of a combination of these two strengths'* (design and craftsmanship)[165] and *'his designs not only surpassed in imaginative quality and originality almost everything which competitors could produce, but they were carried out in glass with a decorative craftsmanship and colouristic genius which was unique.'* [166] There was even a multi-windowed room in the Red House where the glass could be cut and laid out while the lead was inserted to make a finished panel.

However, this was some years in the future and in 1859 Jones did not have the benefit of Morris and his team to help him in his design for the Latin Chapel at Christ Church. The Frideswide window is therefore a completely individual widow, the genius of one mind and unrivalled by his other early designs.

The narrative

How did Burne Jones tell the story? To start with, he had to learn about the legend. Remember that Saint Frideswide had not been talked about for over three hundred years, her saint's day was not celebrated, and knowledge of her life and miracles had nearly melted away. What brought it into the mind of Benjamin Woodward, the architect, to suggest it then is not known, but only a couple of years before Dean Henry Liddell had reinstated some fourteenth-century glass into the windows of the north wall of the Latin chapel, a few yards away from the proposed new window.

Among those images is one that may have stood out as important to the Dean. In the middle of the second window from the west end of the chapel, an indistinct and willowy figure looks out from a pale and beautiful face that hints at an early medieval context. She is wearing a gold crown, suggesting she is from royalty, and is holding a sceptre in her right hand, indicating she has power or jurisdiction over something. She has a blue shawl on her head, which might point to the Virgin Mary and hint that she also is a virgin, and a red cape may symbolise the passion of Christ. A white dress reflects her purity and in her left hand is something that might possibly be a building. Beneath her feet are the words STA FRIDESWIDA. This was the only image of Saint Frideswide that the Cathedral owned, apart from a boss in the chancel, and it had been moved there by

Dean Liddell from its original and now unknown location.

Perhaps Woodward noticed her when he reviewed the chapel, or maybe Dean Liddell suggested it to him when they discussed the project. Whichever man decided on it, they must have felt it was time for Oxford to re-discover its Patron Saint, and the ethereal figure of this enchanting young woman was the perfect starting place.

The most likely source that Jones would have gone to for information on this enigmatic figure was the Monasticon Anglicanum by William Dugdale, a history of the monasteries of England. He was a seventeenth-century historian who collated the history of every pre-reformation monastery in England, with the helpful addition that he wrote in English. His book had been revised and enlarged several times and Oxford had many copies in libraries all over the city. It gives a detailed description of the legend, the formation of the early nunnery and its re-founding as an Augustinian Priory.

Once Jones was clear about the details of the legend, he needed to think of a way of depicting it in stained glass, and we have the good fortune to have not one, but two different cartoons of the window which give us an indication of the design process.

When he visited the Latin Chapel to study the position of the east end window, he would perhaps notice how it catches the morning sun. It is also quite a light chapel, with four windows in its north wall, so he may have been drawn to deeper tones in the glass. More importantly he had to design the space that the stained glass would inhabit in relation to the stonework. Was he going to use the whole area with little stonework, or make separate lights with stone mullions in between?

Then, how could he describe the story? The legend was a narrative with several sequences; should he make Frideswide a static figure on her own, as was usual in fourteenth-century glass, or should he take one of the sequences and fill the whole window with that? But if so, which one? Should he instead try to depict the whole story in several scenes, and how could he present this across the window?

For a new artist, with only three complete windows behind him, this was potent stuff. He may have felt that his future career depended on the way this window turned out, and his two cartoons show how he moved towards the solution he eventually intended to use.

The First Cartoon

In the Aberdeen Art Gallery, Schoolhill, Aberdeen is the first cartoon that Burne Jones painted for the Frideswide window in Christ Church, Oxford. It is a 49cm high and 30cm wide ink and watercolour painting, in a 68.4cm high by 48.2cm wide frame.

The cartoon is in the form of an arched window tightly packed with little scenes. It is divided into 5 horizontal layers, separated by narrow lines, and connected by a sinuous river. There is no sign of stonework, mullions or lead-lines, and its small size and naive detail, suggest it to be a first attempt at making sense of the design. The overall subtle hues of beige, brown, greens and blues, compared to the vibrance of the final widows, also suggest that the darkened varnish has altered the original colours.

The top layer of the design is in the narrow arch at the top of the window and consists of a horizontal watery line with a silhouette of an ox. It is of course the symbol for Oxenford, the old name of Oxford. Below it are two scenes. In the first a little girl is being taught to play the piano by two taller

Burne Jones First Cartoon

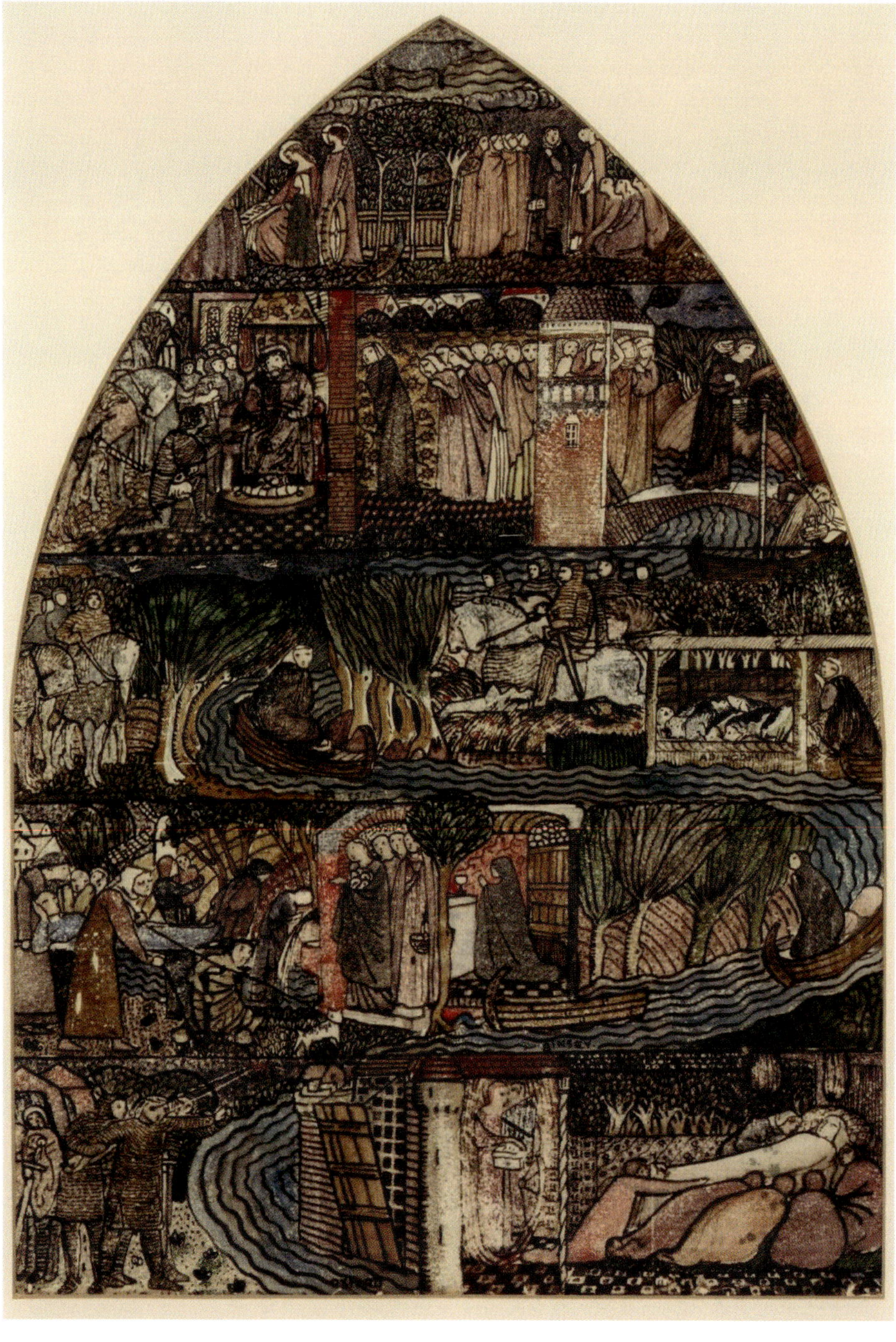

women with halos, one of whom is seated at the piano and the other standing behind holding a large wheel-like object on the ground. This must be a depiction of the childhood of Frideswide, and the two women were Saint Catherine (with the wheel which is her usual symbol) and Saint Cecilia (with the piano indicating her connection with music). They were important to Frideswide in her legend, though their appearance was in a vision at her death, not during her childhood.

The second scene is separated from the first by some wooden fencing and 3 trees and consists of a central figure of a woman carrying something in her right hand and clutching her cloak, surrounded by four women on each side, three of whom are kneeling. This is likely to be a portrayal of Frideswide leaving home to go into the nunnery.

The second layer of the window has three scenes. In the first, an eminent figure is receiving a message from a kneeling figure with two horses in the background. This is Frideswide's father, King Dydan, receiving a proposal of marriage for his daughter from the envoy of King Algar.

The middle scene has a cloaked female figure and eight women listening behind a screen to the king receiving the messenger. This must be Frideswide and her nuns eavesdropping on the proposal. The third scene has the cloaked figure leaving the women in a building and crossing a stone bridge to a small boat, where a white figure awaits her. This must be a depiction of Frideswide escaping to the Thames where a boat and an angel boatman would carry her to safety.

From the second to the fifth layers a sinuous river joins the scenes and must be the River Thames, or Isis as it is known in Oxford, which Jones is using as a device to connect the pictorial narrative. The third layer has four scenes. Starting on the left, the soldiers on horseback are King Algar and his men searching for Frideswide. Then the cloaked figure of Frideswide is on her own, floating down the river in the boat. The third scene is Algar on horseback chasing through the undergrowth with his men, and the fourth scene is Frideswide crouching in a little hut with some animals: probably the pigsty and pigs where the legend says she took refuge.

The fourth layer starts on the right of the window, as the river meanders through the countryside with the lonely Frideswide standing anxiously in her boat. Having left the pigsty behind, she is looking ahead to her next place of retreat. In the middle scene the boat is moored outside a chapel in a wood where Frideswide is kneeling at an altar. This is Binsey, where she settled for three years.

In the final scene of this layer, she is standing at the door of the chapel with three women, her nuns who have joined her. She is welcoming a kneeling man who is all bandaged up with a crutch, as well as a figure on a stretcher and a figure carrying a child. There are other figures and a building in the background. This must be when the villagers heard she was in the wood and came to her for prayers, receiving healing as a result.

The final layer is at the bottom of the window, starting on the left, and shows Algar attempting to cross the river at the portcullis and drawbridge of Oxford, but a thin line from the right ending at his eyes suggests the miraculous blinding as a result of Frideswide's prayers. A small, inserted scene behind the gate towers, shows a faint figure with some other items, which might be Frideswide having returned safely to her monastery, and the last scene is of Frideswide on her deathbed being mourned by her nuns who are all kneeling around her.

It is obvious in this cartoon that Jones had decided to go down the multiple scene option, as he had with his previous two windows, using the Thames as the feature that links the scenes together. However, the way he has presented it is more consistent with a painted collage in the shape of a window than any style of stained glass known to the church and is different from his own previous designs.

As a design for a stained-glass window, it is unlikely that this would work. It is too busy, the scenes are too small, and the colouring is too dark, even allowing for darkening with age, to mention a few artistic problems. It also has no stonework supports except at the sides, and how the glass might have been cut, and where the lead lines might have been placed, is complete conjecture. It has all the features of a painting on canvas rather than a window design and, without solid stone mullions, the stained glass would have been too fragile to stay together once inserted in the stone window-embrasure.

One way this design would have worked is as a tapestry, embroidery or appliqué in the form of a long collage around the walls of a room similar to, though not in the same style as, the Bayeaux tapestry.

However, its small size suggests it was just a trial, not a full-size cartoon from which a craftsman could work, and it is highly likely that if he showed it to Powell's, they would have rejected it on the grounds that it was unworkable. However, the basic details of the scenes are familiar, as many of them are reproduced in the finished window, and we will see in the second cartoon how Burne Jones achieved this change.

But how had the cartoon got to the Aberdeen Art Gallery?

Provenance of the first cartoon

On enquiry, the cartoon was purchased by the Aberdeen Art Gallery from a Mrs E C Robichaud in 1949. How it had got to Scotland, so far from London where Burne-Jones lived and worked, and who Mrs Robichaud was, were mysteries that needed to be solved.

Further research into the Aberdeen Art Gallery catalogue of collections revealed that it had been in the private collection of a William Llewellyn Hacon and passed to his widow, a Mrs E C Robichaud (by her second marriage), before being purchased in 1949 by the Aberdeen Art Gallery. Who Llwellyn Hacon was required more detailed research, as no biography of him has been written. Piecing together information from several internet sources has revealed more, and a possible line of transmission.

William Llewellyn Hacon 1860-1910 was a contemporary of Sir Edward Burne-Jones. Although he was twenty-seven years younger, he died only twelve years after him. He was a lawyer who became a wealthy barrister and patron of the arts.[167] His second wife was a beautiful model, born in 1874 as Edith Catherine Broadbent, but known as Amaryllis, or Ryllis for short. She was in London in the 1890s as an artist's model and had *'the rich golden hair and voluptuous figure associated with Titian and the later works of Dante Gabriel Rossetti.'* [168] She soon became a high-class escort, associating with the top painters and artists of the day,[169] rather like Elizabeth Siddall and Annie Miller, the muses respectively of Dante Gabriel Rossetti and Holman Hunt some years before. However, there is no evidence she was known to Morris or Burne Jones, who were by then towards the end of their careers.

Hacon, a wealthy barrister and art collector, admired a pastel of Amaryllis that had been drawn by Charles Haselwood Shannon, which he bought. He then asked to meet the original, and promptly fell in love. They married in 1895 and she took the name of Ryllis Llewellyn Hacon, becoming a society hostess. Hacon used some of his money to finance the publishing company Vale Press from 1896 to 1904 with Charles Ricketts, which was named after Ricketts's home, Vale House in Chelsea. The Hacons moved into

Vale House sometime after 1896, not long before Burne Jones died, in 1898, and probably acquired the cartoon during this period, either in Burne Jones' lifetime or soon after his death.

Hacon also loved golf and built a home called Oversteps in Dornoch, north-east Scotland (now Oversteps Care Home), and he must have transferred much of his art collection there. He died in 1910 when Ryllis was only 36. She then threw herself into public life, in particular the Women's Suffrage Movement.[170] With the outbreak of war she volunteered to go to Royaumont Hospital in France as an orderly, becoming housekeeper there between 1915 and 1917.[171]

During the war she met Canadian soldier William Robichaud. They married in 1918 and she reverted to her real name of Edith Catherine. After the war they settled in Dornoch[172] and adopted two boys. By 1931, she became an active member of the community, particularly in the Dornoch Girl Guides.[173]

Aberdeen Art Gallery has over nineteen items that were bought from Mrs Robichaud in 1949, which include the Burne Jones cartoon. She would have been around 75 years old then and may have been facing the end of her life. Since the children were adopted into her second marriage and had nothing to do with Hacon, she may have felt that they had no reason to want the whole collection after her death, so offered a number of the works to the Aberdeen Art Gallery.

This is probably the route the first Frideswide window cartoon took in its path to the Aberdeen Art Gallery, and it is amazing that it survived at all. However, the second cartoon series is something else. Treasured by their various owners as works of art in themselves, they are displayed in a very special room in a place that is again almost as remote from Burne Jones himself as the first cartoon.

The Final Cartoons

In the stunning Council Meeting Chamber of the Cheltenham Ladies' College, hung high up on the walls, is a series of eight full-colour cartoons of the Saint Frideswide window at Christ Church Cathedral, Oxford.

The archives of the College record that they are painted in oils on canvas, and are framed and glazed, each canvas being 6ft. by 2ft. 7in. and each framed picture is 6ft, 5in by 2ft 11in. They are the final cartoons painted by Burne Jones and would have been the actual representations used by the glass craftsmen of Powell's to create the window.

Though their choice of setting is magnificent and worthy of these exceptional panels, they are hung well above normal head height and, being darkened with age, they are quite difficult to see properly.

The panels are also covered in glass, and the windows and lights in the room reflect on the surface of the glass, obscuring the paintings beneath. They really need to be viewed in daylight, with all the windows obscured by gauze to prevent reflections. The top of a stepladder would be a useful viewing platform, and binoculars would make the details more accessible. However, when these difficulties are overcome, preferably by studying a really good professional photograph, they begin to look amazing and better than the stained-glass equivalents in Christ Church Cathedral.

Provenance of the final cartoons

On first viewing these wonderful paintings, which are real treasures in themselves, questions crowd into the mind. Where did these cartoons come from? Who owned them after Burne-Jones? How did they get to be hanging at Cheltenham Ladies' College, a place unconnected with the artist?

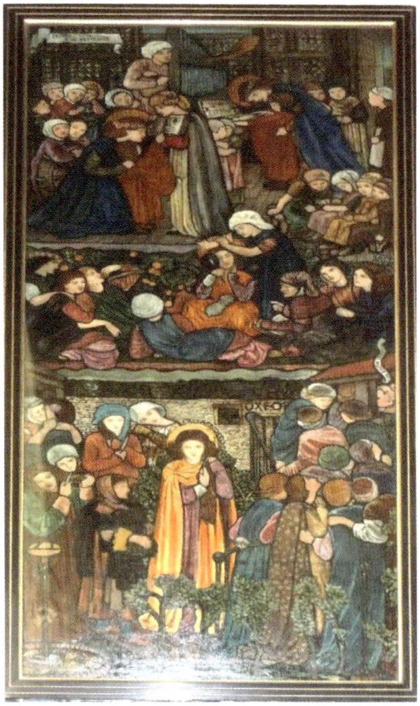

Panel 1

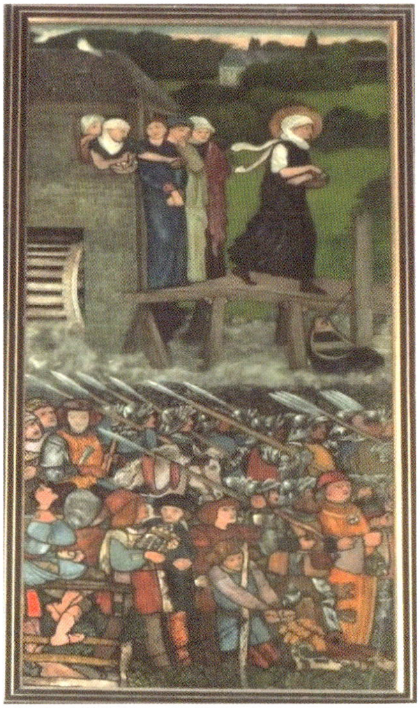

Panel 3

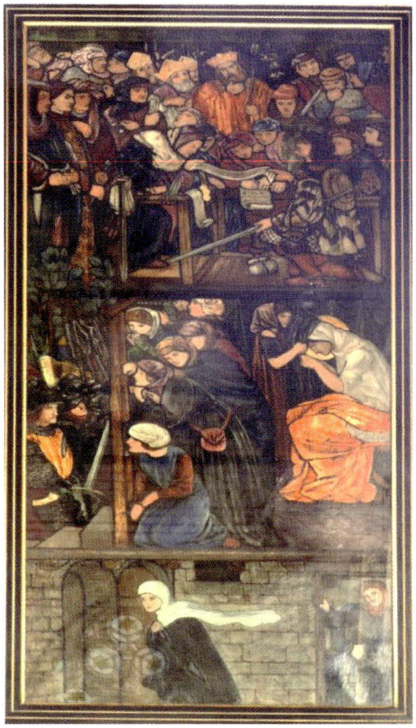

Panel 2

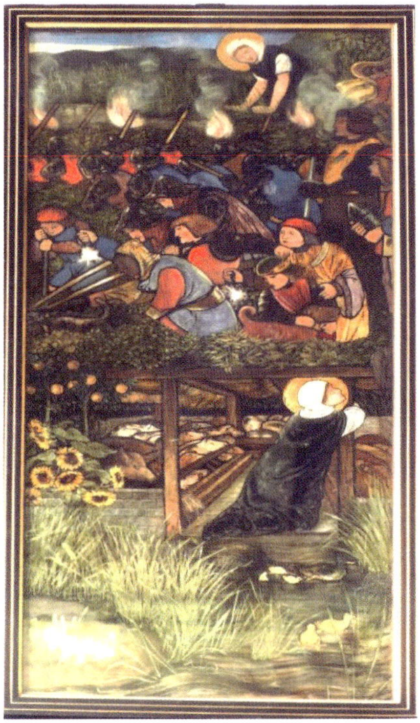

Panel 4

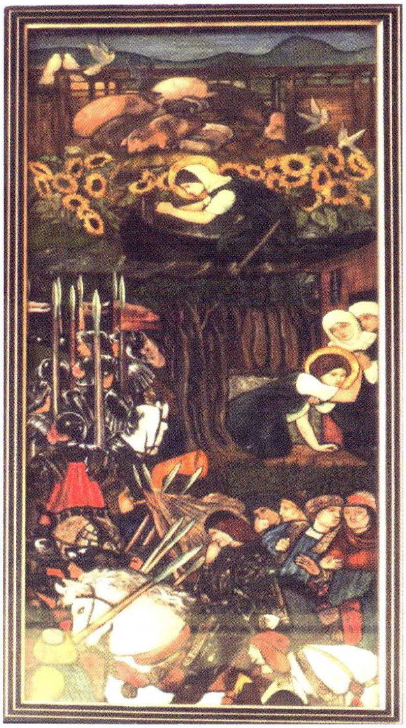

Panel 5

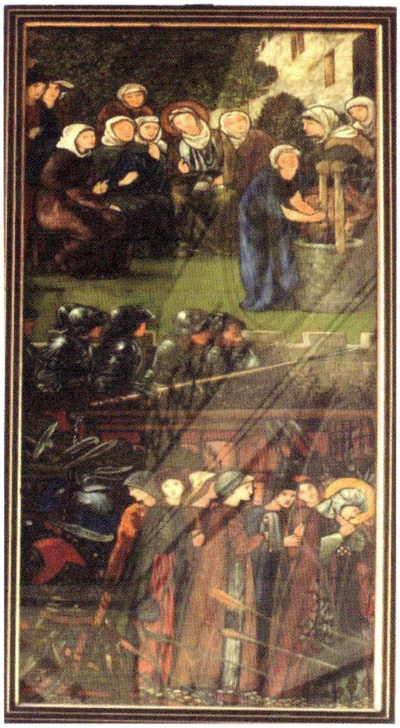

Panel 7

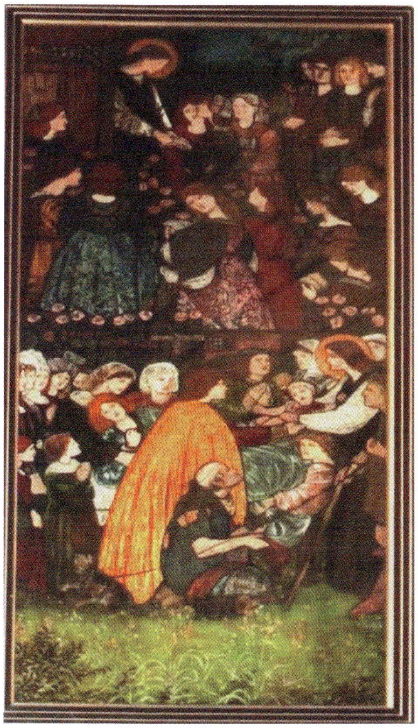

Panel 6

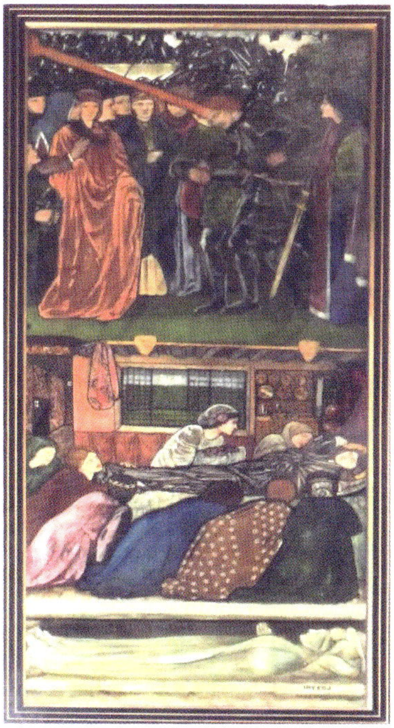

Panel 8

Christopher Wood's book, Burne Jones, gives us a first clue when, on describing the Saint Frideswide windows it says, '*Burne Jones made the cartoons into a screen, which he kept in his studio until 1865, when he sold it to Birket Foster.*' [174] Why and how did he make them into a screen, and who was Birket Foster?

Wikipedia gives a good summery of the man: Myles Birket Foster 1825-1899, a direct contemporary of Burne Jones, was a '*popular and successful illustrator and water colour artist*.'[175] He was an acquaintance of Dante Gabriel Rossetti who probably introduced him to William Morris.[176]

In the early 1860s Birket Foster bought some land in the village of Witley, near Godalming in Surrey to build a house which he mostly designed himself and called The Hill. He was one of the first people to employ the firm of Morris and Co. to do the interior decoration[177] and, in the process, he met Burne Jones. Birket Foster was steeped in the same medievalism that inspired William Morris and was genuinely receptive of the work of this new company. His new house was soon full of the stained glass, decorations, and embroidery of this new firm.[178]

So how and why did the cartoons end up as a screen? Burne Jones had married Georgina McDonald in 1860 and was very busy developing his working relationship with William Morris, Val Prinsep, Charlie Faulkner and George Watts, who would be early partners in the firm of Morris and Co. from 1861.

They started married life at Jones' flat in 24 Russell Place, London, but spent some time at the Red House at Bexleyheath with Morris and his wife Janey where they joined in to decorate it in the medieval style they all loved.[179] In 1861 they moved to 62 Great Russell St, where he did some of his work, but the Morris firm moved its workshop and studio into 8 Red Lion Square later that year.[180] The Jones's existence was hand-to-mouth to say the least, and where he could have kept his huge cartoons is unknown, unless they were with William Morris or at the studios in Red Lion Square.[181]

Jones was working hard on various projects when in 1864 he was encouraged by Ruskin to apply for membership of the Association of the Royal Water-Colour Society. He appears to have met Birket Foster in connection with this,[182] and struck up a friendship, as well as working on Foster's commissions to Morris and Co. for decorations in his home in Witley, one of their first commissions. Four pictures of St George and the Dragon[183] were definitely painted by Jones for Foster around this time.[184]

In October 1864, the Jones's lost a baby at only 3 weeks old when the family went down with scarlet fever, and this unsettled them so much that Jones is

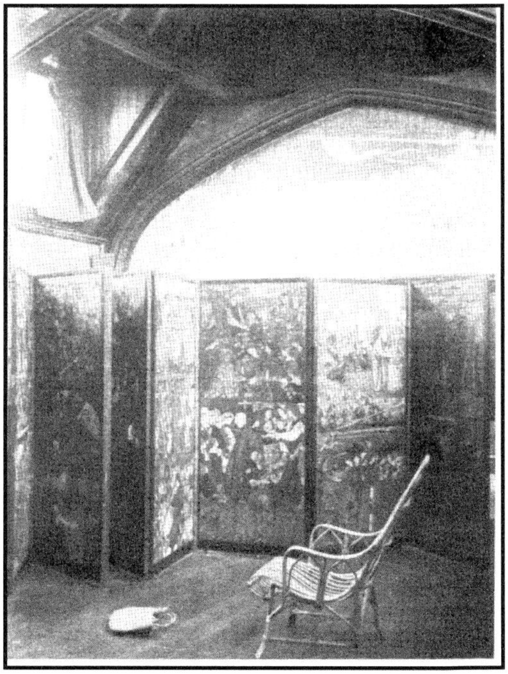

Frideswide cartoon panels made up as screen

recorded as having no work between August 1864 and March 1865.[185] They went to recuperate in Hastings, but Georgie could not bear to return to Great Russell St, so Ned rented 41 Kensington Sq. and moved their belongings before she returned.[186] He had a studio in two of the rooms. [187]

The screen might have been put together during these early years of marriage as a means of dividing his large rooms into smaller multifunction apartments, but it must also have been during this troubling and difficult time that Birket Foster offered to relieve Jones of his huge masterpiece. [188]

Morris and Janey also moved from the Red House to Queen Square, Bloomsbury in the autumn of 1865, [189] so if they had been housing the screen for Jones it needed a new home.

In the Cheltenham Ladies' College archives is also a photograph of the eight cartoon panels made into a screen, the very screen mentioned in Wood's book. It is standing at the end of a large hall against a masonry wall, and above it is an arched timber beam and a wooden beamed roof structure. In front of it is a casually placed cane garden chair without cushions, with a white bag on the floor in front of the chair. The whole impression is of neglect, as though the room, though magnificent, is little used. A paper describes the photograph.

> *'Photograph dated about 1880,*
> *and taken at The Hill, Witley, Surrey, while*
> *the item was in the possession of*
> *Birket Foster, R.W.S.*
> *Original of photograph now in the possession*
> *of Sarah G. A. Glasson,*
> *grand-daughter of Birket Foster.'*

A further copy of the photograph is in Jan Reynolds book, Birket Foster, which describes how an extension was built to The Hill in 1866 which included a billiard room, also used as an oil painting studio.[190] Jan Reynolds seems to suggest that this room may have been especially built to house the Frideswide screens, which had been acquired in 1865, only six years or so after they were painted.

At over 6ft tall and 2ft wide, the eight panels made a very lengthy and bulky screen. Birket Foster probably used the billiard room as his studio at first, but it was later used for amateur theatricals and the screen may have come in handy to shield a dressing area. Perhaps over time the room was used less and less, hence the appearance of neglect. A paper in the archives of the Cheltenham Ladies' College tells us how the panels were acquired by Birket Foster.

'SIR EDWARD BURNE-JONES (1833-1898) *designed many famous stained-glass windows for his friend William Morris who had been a fellow undergraduate with him at Oxford University, but the S. Frideswide window in Christ Church Cathedral was one of Burne-Jones first designs for stained glass and was carried out by Messrs Powell in about the year 1860* (actually 1858). *From 1861 Burne-Jones, in his stained-glass designs, worked exclusively for William Morris.*

The S. Frideswide window in Christ Church is not nearly so effective as the large designs in colour for it, because the architect made an unfortunate mistake in calculating the dimensions. The eight large cartoons painted in oils for the window represent Burne-Jones' most splendid work in originality of planning and decorative effect. They depict sixteen incidents in the life of S. Frideswide. Burne-Jones framed the eight panels into a screen which adorned his studio.

His fellow artist, Birket Foster, the watercolour painter, saw the screen in 1863 in the artist's studio and begged to be allowed to purchase it, but Burne-Jones was not willing to part with it at that time. Later, in 1865, when Burne-Jones moved to another studio, he let Birket Foster have the screen, which then adorned Birket Foster's home in Witley (Surrey) until it was bought from him by Graham Robertson. Graham Robertson then detached the eight large panels from the screen and framed each separately in a narrow band of black under Burne-Jones' direction. Graham Robertson writes of them in his book 'Time Was' and refers to them as 'those lovely panels, perhaps the most spontaneous and fascinating of all the works of Burne-Jones and far finer than the window for which they were designed.' [191]

In the archives of the college is confirmation that the panels came through Walford Graham Robertson,[192] in a paper dated 27th January 1950.

'In memory of W Graham Robertson (1866-1948), Painter – Poet – Playwright, his executors R A Wooding and Kerrison Preston have presented his favourite Saint Frideswide panels by Burne-Jones to Cheltenham Ladies' College to be hung in the ~~Library~~ Music Room as a decoration and inspiration.'

A note explains *'One of the executors, I think Kerrison Preston, visited the library and agreed that the panelled background would not do the St Frideswide panels justice, and that the warm walls of the Music Room set them off far better,'* signed T M H (unknown name). [193]

However, the panels are not now in the Music Room either. A note in Jan Reynolds' book states, *'In 1950, the St Frideswide panels were presented by the executors of W. G. Robertson to Cheltenham Ladies' College. These paintings are much valued by the College and in 1983-4 are scheduled to be removed from their present site in the Music Wing to a more prominent position in the Council Meeting Chamber.'*[194] That is where they remain to this day.

The Cheltenham Ladies' College Magazine for 1950 also gives a résumé of the panels.

BURNE-JONES PANELS

'The most outstanding gift of the year was the presentation of the original design painted in oils by Sir Edward Burne-Jones for his St Frideswide stained-glass window in Christ Church, Oxford. The designs were in the possession of W Graham Robertson and have been given in memory of him by his executors, Mr Kerrison Preston and Mr R A Wooding.

There are eight panels framed in black and gold, depicting sixteen scenes in the life of St Frideswide, who lived in the eighth century A.D. and was the legendary foundress and patron saint of Oxford. She renounced the world and founded a nunnery at Oxford where she lived and devoted herself to prayer. A neighbouring prince, Alfgar, wanted to marry her and tried to seize her by force, but she escaped in a boat down the Isis and after many adventures, during the course of which she performed miracles and at one stage took refuge in a pigsty, the prince abandoned his pursuit and St Frideswide was able to return peaceably to her nunnery. The scenes depicted by Burne- Jones are mostly connected with her flight from Prince Alfgar.

The St Frideswide window was one of Burne-Jones' first designs for stained glass carried out in about 1860. The designs are far better than the window as the architect made an unfortunate mistake in calculating the dimensions which resulted in the panels being too big for it and causing it to look over-crowded. They represent some of the artist's finest work in originality of planning and decorative effect and make a really lovely furnishing for the walls of the newly painted Music Room, round which they have been hung.

The donors expressed the wish that "the students of Cheltenham Ladies' College, who are on their way to Oxford or any other university for further work, may follow the Lady Frideswide in her sense of vocation and her strength of purpose, undeflected by prince or pigs!"' [195]

The donor of the painted panels was therefore a W Graham Robertson and his memoirs Time Was do give further details as to his connection with Burne-Jones, as well as a remarkable little story about how the panels were almost altered irredeemably by Burne-Jones himself. [196]

GRAHAM ROBERTSON writes

'His (Burne-Jones') pictures had always appealed to me strongly, but more especially his early work, so colourful, so steeped in romantic suggestion, and I had been lucky in securing most beautiful examples in the eight panels setting forth the life of Saint Frideswide, painted very early in his career as designs for a great window in Christ Church Cathedral, Oxford.

Those lovely panels, perhaps the most spontaneous and fascinating of all his works and far finer than the window for which they were designed, were made into a screen by the artist and were for long in his home in Kensington Square, until his friend Birket Foster, persuaded him to part with them and bore them off to 'The Hill' in Witley, which already boasted stained glass by the same hand and a series of decorative paintings from the history of Saint George.... The great Frideswide screen stood in a seldom-used studio, and I finally induced Birket Foster to pass it on to me; when I detached the panels, framing each separately in a narrow band of black under Burne-Jones' direction.'

He goes on, *'Then came a difficulty which nearly always occurs when an artist comes across his own early work after losing sight of it for many years. He at once wished to restore and repaint. Now this puts the owner of the picture into a very awkward position. It would seem ungracious, nay unfair, to deny to the creator of a picture the right to work his will on it, yet to deliver it into his hands is to court disaster.*

If a picture actually wants re-touching in order, for instance, to hide an accidental injury, the artist who produced it many years ago is the last man who should be allowed to touch it, because, quite erroneously, he imagines himself still to be the man who painted it, and therefore falls upon it without mercy or respect. No artist should be allowed to see a picture painted by himself more than twenty years ago.'

He continues: *'Charles Hallé once told me of a miserable day spent at the Grosvenor Gallery during the hanging of the Millais Exhibition, while Millais completely repainted one of his early works to its utter and hopeless undoing. To watch the earnest young work disappearing under layers of slick commonplace was unforgettably sad.'*

He goes on, *'I fought for my panels. "There's hardly anything to be done," I pleaded. "Only those little joins to be painted over. Let me do it. Let us get a man from Whiteley's to do it. Don't let us do it all - but please don't do it yourself!" Burne-Jones was kind but quite firm too. I was respectful (I hope) but quite firm. I left town for a few days and Burne-Jones raided the house in my absence, carrying off four panels. I, on my return, raided the Grange and got all the panels back again. Finally, under stress of other work, the painter forgot about the matter and six of the eight panels remain in their original condition. These lovely works are amongst my most cherished treasures, but dearer still is the memory of their creator and the great gift of his friendship.'* [197]

Graham Robertson went to live at Witley in 1888,[198] and he must have acquired the panels sometime between then and 1894 when The Hill was sold by Birket Foster due to ill health. The use by Robertson of the phrase *'I finally induced Birket Foster to pass it on to me'* [199] might suggest that some time had passed since he first began the negotiations and that it was nearer to 1894 than 1888. Despite his apparent neglect of the panels, Birket Foster must have been exceptionally fond of them.

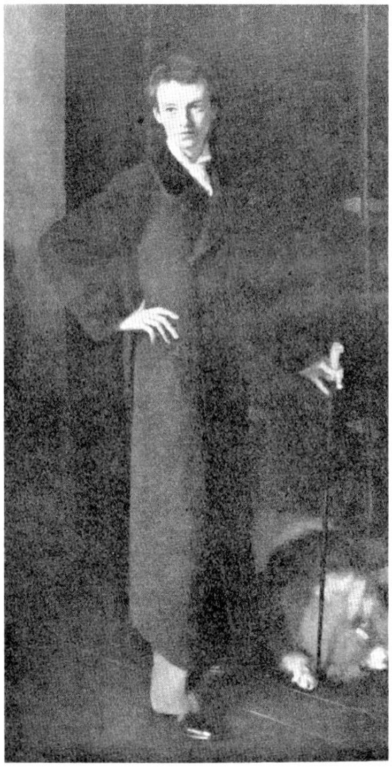

W Graham Robertson from his book Time Was

Jan Reynolds gives some illumination to this in her book Birket Foster. *'In 1893 Birket Foster became seriously ill with what were probably the first symptoms of his last illness'* and he realised he needed to move to a smaller place.[200] *'Because he could not house his remaining artwork, he sold much of it through Christie's in April 1894.'* [201] The screen was so large and unwieldy that he would certainly not have been able to accommodate it in a smaller house. The panels were saved from the open market by this private purchase, but Birket Foster must have only been induced to part with them by necessity.

The house that Graham Robertson moved to was called Sandhills and he bought it from the artist Helen Allingham and her husband William. He related in his book **Time Was** that *'The house was old-fashioned when we came to it that autumn morning more than forty years ago; now it is pre-historic, and to-day I take a foolish pride in its including no electric light, no telephone, no garage (and no motor in it), no central heating, and no bathroom....'* [202]

A house of this description does not sound as though it could accommodate so large an item as the Frideswide screen, and its bulk and weight must have been the reason why Graham Robertson separated it into individual pictures. It would have been the only way to make them manageable. He does not describe where he kept the separated panels, but he owned them for well over 50 years from 1894 to his death in 1948.

This was, of course during the time when Burne-Jones' work had lost its popularity and shows Graham Robinson's high regard for these unique works, but he must have been unsure how to dispose of them after his death. Why a single man, without children, wanted to donate them to Cheltenham Ladies' College a long way from his home, is a mystery. I made an application for a copy of his will in case it held any other information about the circumstances, but it does not appear to have survived, so no further light could be shed on the decision by the man himself, unless of course the decision was not made by Graham Robinson at all, but by his executors. We know only their names, and one of them may have had a connection with the college and felt it was the best place to preserve the cartoons. We will never be completely sure.

Comparing the Cartoons with the Finished Window

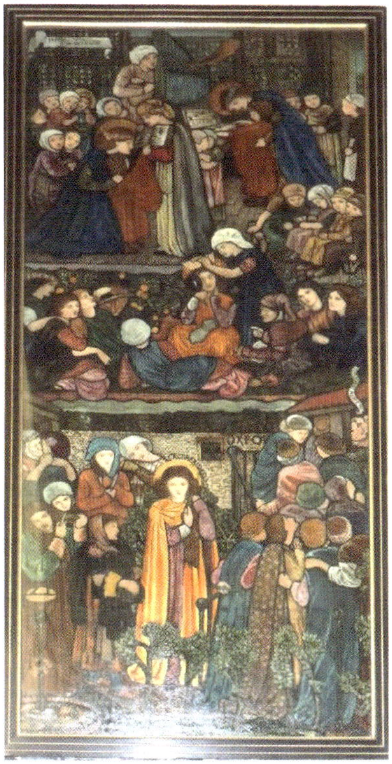

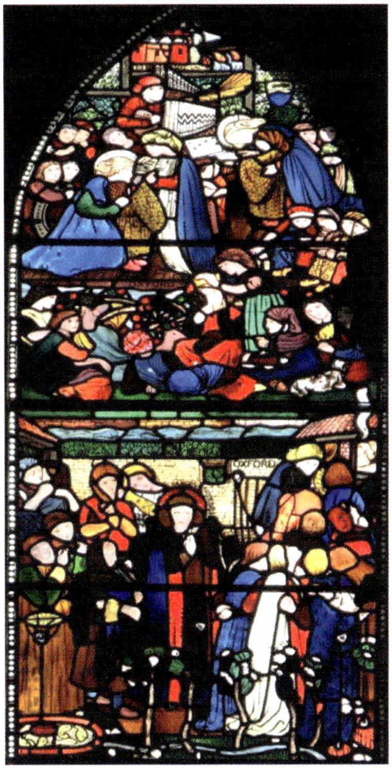

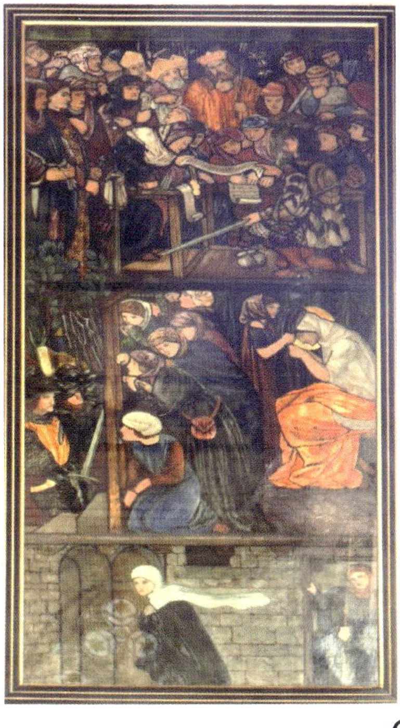

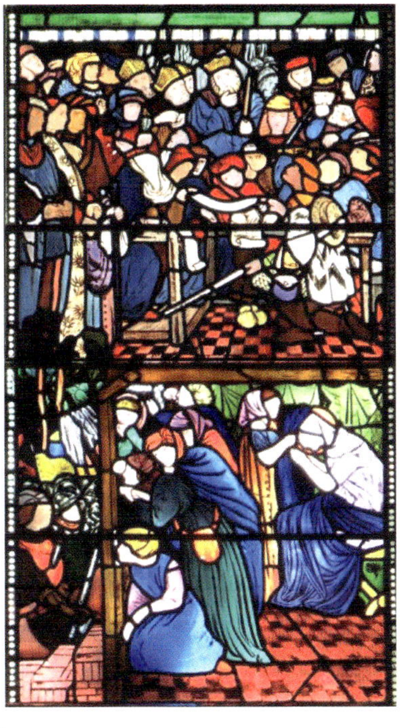

Column 1

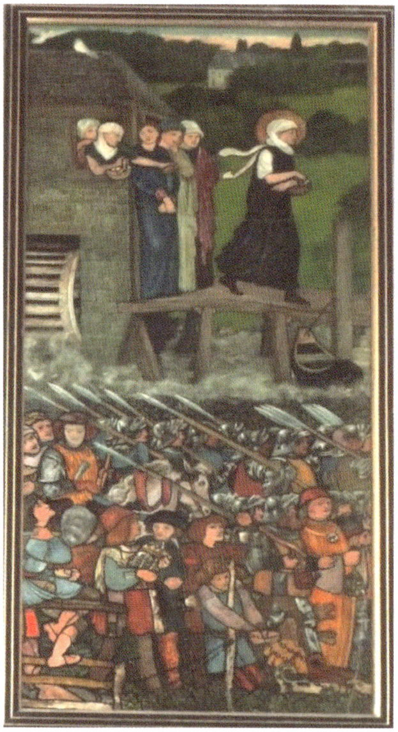

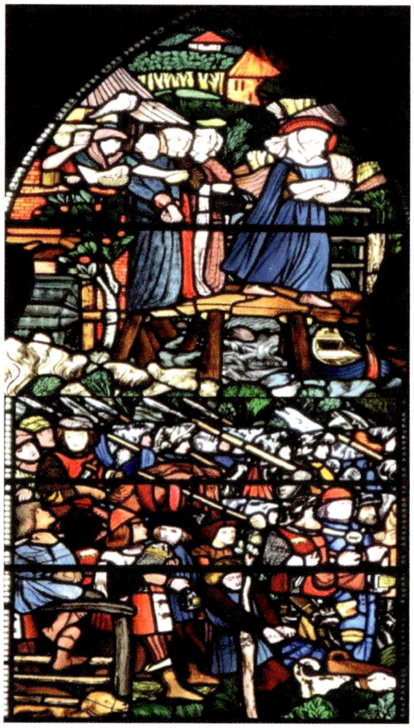

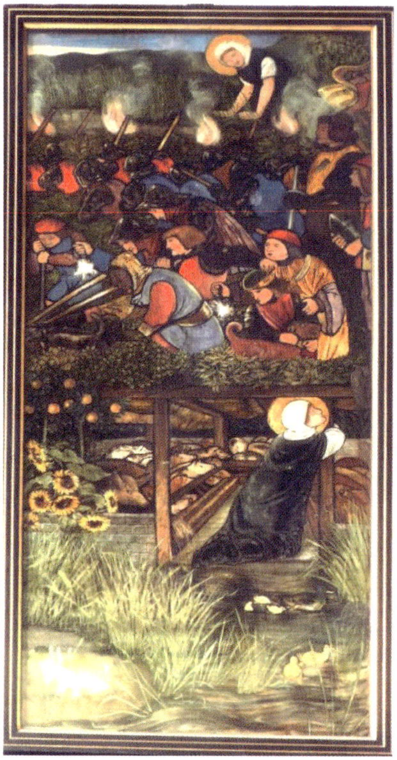

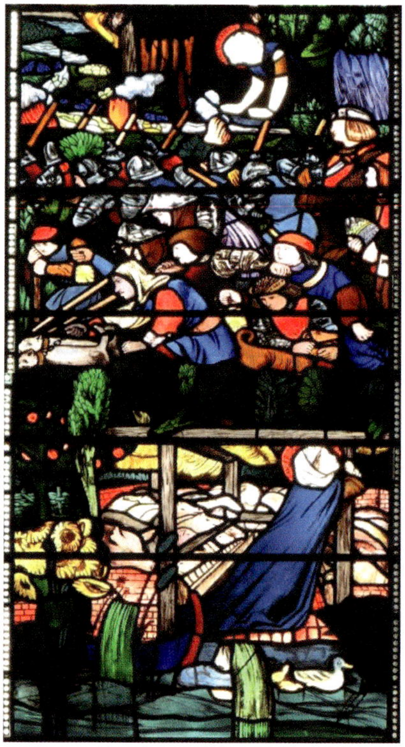

Column 2

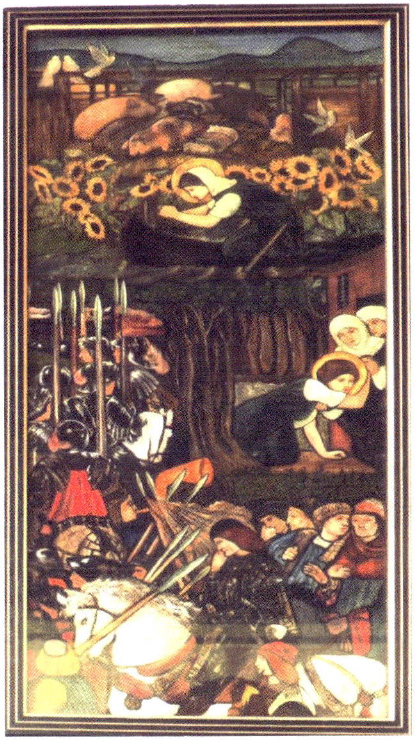

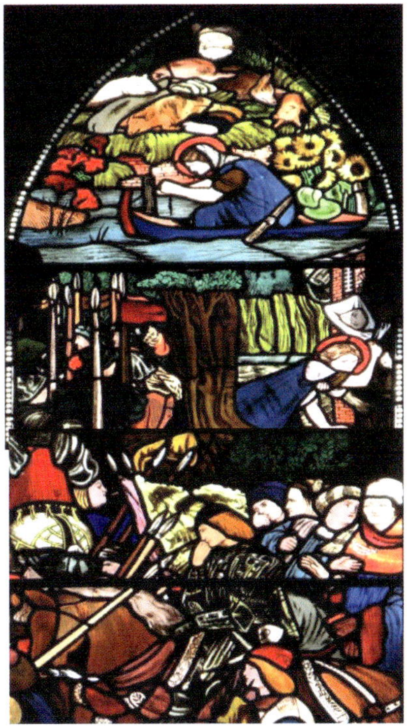

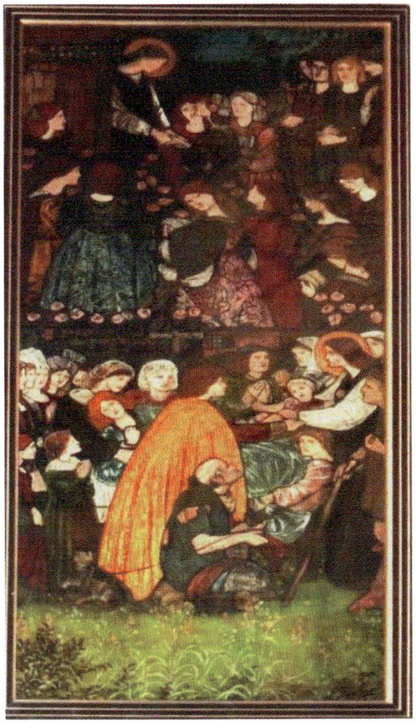

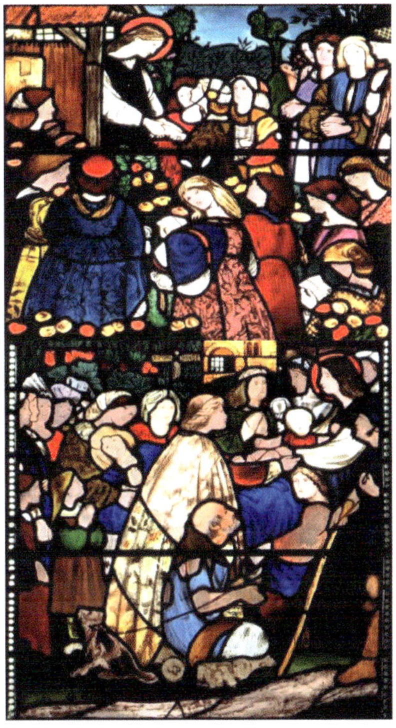

Column 3

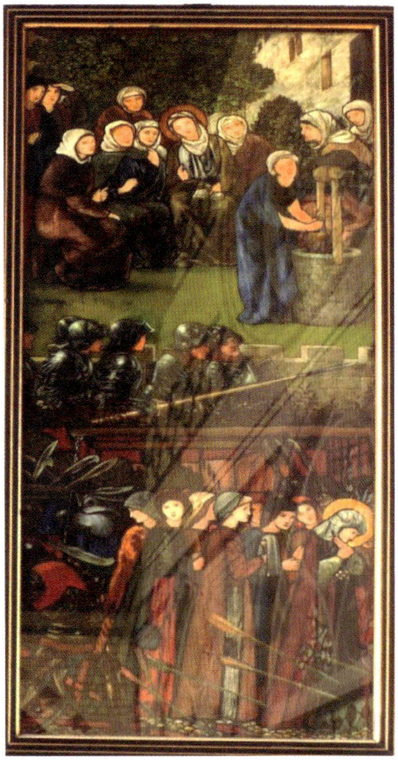

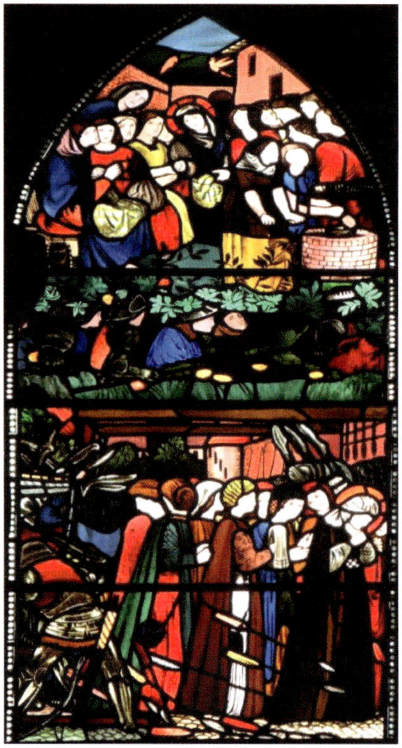

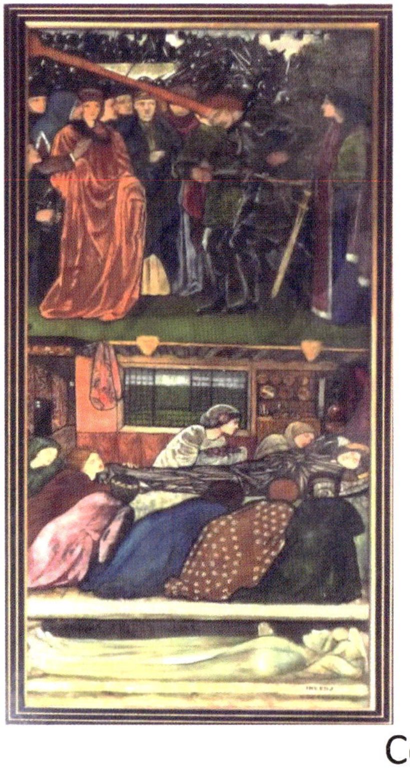

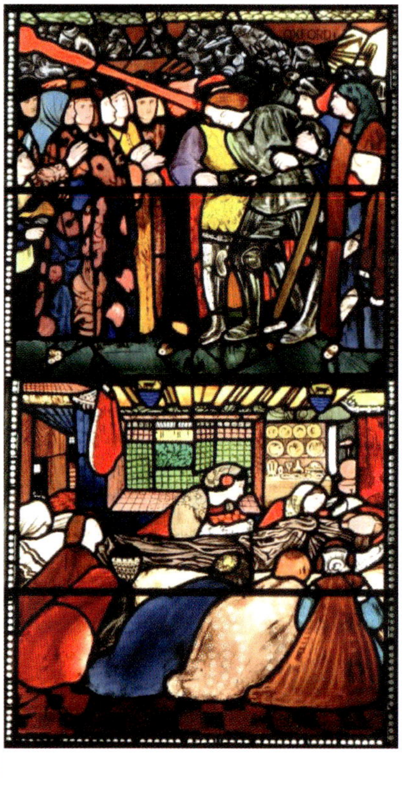

Column 4

Summary

So that is the story of the Frideswide window cartoons. In most other stained-glass designs, the cartoons would have been kept by the firm which commissioned the work. Why Powell's released the designs back to Burne Jones is still a mystery. It may have been something to do with the mistaken measurements that had caused the design to be altered and upset Jones so much when he saw the final window. He did, in fact, suggest re-doing it at this own expense.

Perhaps he wanted to be reminded of the beauty of his original conception, not the discomfort of the finished work. Making them into a screen for his studio was a good use for them and would enable him, and others, to view the real thing at eye-level. They certainly inspired Birkett Foster and Graham Robertson to honour their beauty and originality, and the place where they now reside is a fitting tribute to their remarkable creator.

However, a thought should be given to the stained-glass manufacturers who translated the cartoons into the finished glass window. Comparison of the window's panels with the cartoons will quickly show that the glass cutters added a great deal of artistic acumen to the finished product, and it was their genius that renders the windows such a coherent and pleasing entity. It was they who realised the potential of a young artist with bags of talent but little experience and helped to put him on the road to greatness.

A Last Word

Of the many wonderful treasures to be found in Christ Church Cathedral, Oxford, all of which have stories to tell, the Frideswide window must be somewhere near, if not at, the top. But the story the window tells must surpass most other stories in the cathedral as it is the foundation story of Oxford itself.

In the depth of the Dark Ages, a young girl is presented with a new and exciting faith. She embraces it whole-heartedly, taking on all its ideals, and puts God at the top of her personal agenda. Her life is a shining light that cannot be kept hidden in an obscure monastery.

Today the morning lights sends a sunburst of colours streaming from her window, illuminating the shrine, and casting a mosaic of colour onto the floor (see page 30). It is like a vision of the light of God that shone into Frideswide's heart and is still shining for us today.

Appendix

Early Burne Jones stained-glass windows

Date	Stained glass manufacturer	Church / Location	Window
1857	Levers and Barraud	St Columba's Church Topcliffe, North Yorkshire.	Annunciation panel: the left hand of a three-light window, the other lights being Visitation and Nativity by Michael F Halliday.
1857	James Powell and Sons	Former King Street Congregational Church, Maidstone, Kent.	The Good Shepherd, single panel window, now in Birmingham Art Gallery.
1857	James Powell and Sons	Bradfield College, near Reading, Berkshire. Dining hall.	Three-light window: Adam and Eve after the fall, the Tower of Babel, Solomon and Sheba.
1858	James Powell and Sons	Christ Church Cathedral, Oxford. Latin Chapel.	The four-light St Frideswide window. Commissioned 1858, erected 1859.
1859-60	James Powell and Sons	Holy Cross and St Lawrence Church, Waltham Abbey, Essex.	The Tree of Jesse, in the three-light east window. Also, the Days of Creation rose window in tracery above. Erected 1860-61.
1862-63	Morris and Co.	St Helen's Church Darley Dale, Derbyshire.	Song of Solomon.
1863	Morris and Co.	St Michael's and All Angels Church, Lyndhurst, Hampshire.	South transept four-light window of Joshua staying the sun and moon, Elijah and the priests of Baal, the Stoning of St Stephen and the Liberation of St Peter.

Bibliography

1. **Archives of Christ Church Cathedral.** Letter by Burne-Jones about window.

2. **Oxford, The Cathedral and See** by Percy Dearmer. Published by George Bell and Sons 1899.

3. **Oxford Cathedral** S A Warner. SPCK 1924.

4. **Pevsner Oxfordshire 2002**, Jennifer Sherwood.

5. **Burne-Jones and William Morris in Oxford and the Surrounding Area**, Ann S Dean BA AKC Published by Heritage Press, Malvern.

6. **English Heritage in Stained Glass Oxford**, Archer/Crewe/Cormack.

7. **Wikipedia** Edward Burne-Jones .

8. **Edward Burne-Jones** by Penelope Fitzgerald. Sutton Publishing 2003.

9. **Burne-Jones** by Christopher Wood. Published by Weidenfeld and Nicolson 1998.

10. **The Stained Glass of William Morris and his Circle,** A Charles Sewter. Published by Yale University Press 1974.

11. **King's Guide to the Cathedrals of England 1862, Oxford Cathedral,** p27.

12. Search internet under William Llwellyn Hacon or Edith Hacon for History Links Archive, and History Links Dornoch

13. www.scarletfinders.co.uk/139.html.

14.https://en.wikipedia.org/wiki/Edith_Hacon Search other links for Charles Ricketts and Vale Press.

15. **Archives** of Cheltenham Ladies' College.

16. **Time Was**: **the reminiscences of W Graham Robertson.** Publisher: Hamish Hamilton, 1945 edition.

17**. Letters to Katie** from Edward Burne-Jones with introduction by W Graham Robertson Macmillan 1925.

18. **Birket Foster by Jan Reynolds**, 1984, B T Batsford Ltd London.

19. **Myles Birket Foster,** http://en.wikipedia.org/wiki/Myles_Birket_Foster.

20. **Edward Burne-Jones, David Peters Corbett** 2004 Tate Publishing a division of Tate enterprises Ltd, Millbank, London SW1P 4RG www.tate.org.uk.

21 **A History of Bradfield College** 1850-1875, a copy held at Bradfield College.

22 **Oxoniensia** 2020 Vol 85 article p125

References (above book, page, number)

---

[1] 22 **Oxoniesia 2020** vol 85
[2] 3 **Oxford Cathedral** S A Warner p 39
[3] 1 **Archives of Christ Church**
[4] 1 **Archives of Christ Church**
[5] 2 **Oxford Cathedral** Percy Dearmer p108
[6] 1 **Archives of Christ Church**
[7] 2 **Oxford Cathedral** Percy Dearmer p105
[8] 2 **Oxford Cathedral** Percy Dearmer p106
[9] 8 **Edward Burne-Jones** P Fitzgerald p37
[10] 3 **Oxford Cathedral** S A Warner p105
[11] 8 **Edward Burne-Jones** P Fitzgerald p12
[12] 8 " p16
[13] 8 **Edward Burne-Jones** P Fitzgerald p18
[14] 8 " p32
[15] 8 " p21
[16] 8 " p21

[17] 8 " p30
[18] 8 " p37
[19] 8 " p32
[20] 8 " p36
[21] 2 **Oxford Cathedral** Percy Dearmer p105
[22] 8 **Edward Burne-Jones** P Fitzgerald p44
[23] 8 " p48
[24] 8 " p48
[25] 10 **Stained Glass** A Charles Sewter p14
[26] 8 **Edward Burne-Jones** P Fitzgerald p51
[27] 2 **Oxford Cathedral** Percy Dearmer p105
[28] 9 **Burne-Jones** Christopher Wood p23
[29] 4 **Pevsner Oxfordshire 2002** p119
[30] 9 **Burne-Jones** Christopher Wood p23
[31] 8 **Edward Burne-Jones** P Fitzgerald p51
[32] 8 " p56
[33] 8 " p59
[34] 8 " p58
[35] 10 **Stained Glass** A Charles Sewter
[36] 10 "
[37] 20 **Edward Burne-Jones** Corbett p21
[38] 20 " p21
[39] 20 " p21
[40] 8 **Edward Burne-Jones** P Fitzgerald p51
[41] 21 **A History of Bradfield College** Ch2
[42] 9 **Burne-Jones** Christopher Wood p24
[43] 20 **Edward Burne-Jones** Corbett p16
[44] 8 **Edward Burne-Jones** P Fitzgerald p13
[45] 21 **A History of Bradfield College** p12
[46] 10 **Stained Glass** A Charles Sewter p15
[47] 10 **Stained Glass** A Charles Sewter p14
[48] 9 **Burne-Jones** Christopher Wood p23
[49] 9 " p21
[50] 9 " p22
[51] 3 **Oxford Cathedral** S A Warner p96
[52] 8 **Edward Burne-Jones** P Fitzgerald p29, p48
[53] 2 **Oxford Cathedral** Percy Dearmer p106
[54] 2 " p106
[55] 11 **King's Guide to Cathedrals 1862** p27
[56] 1 **Archives of Christ Church**
[57] 10 **Stained Glass** A Charles Sewter p17
[58] 10 " p23
[59] 5 **Burne-Jones in Oxford** Ann S Dean p19
[60] 3 **Oxford Cathedral** S A Warner p95
[61] 10 **Stained Glass** A Charles Sewter p15
[62] 10 " p18
[63] 10 " p15
[64] 10 " p28
[65] 10 " p15
[66] 10 " p29
[67] 10 " p29
[68] 10 " p15
[69] 10 " p15
[70] 2 **Oxford Cathedral** Percy Dearmer p106
[71] 2 " p106
[72] 6 **English Heritage in Stained Glass** p47
[73] 3 **Oxford Cathedral** S A Warner p95
[74] 2 **Oxford Cathedral** Percy Dearmer p106
[75] 9 **Burne-Jones** Christopher Wood p24
[76] 9 " p24
[77] 5 **Burne-Jones in Oxford** Ann S Dean p16
[78] 10 **Stained Glass** A Charles Sewter p8
[79] 10" p8
[80] 5 **Burne-Jones in Oxford** Ann S Dean p16
[81] 10 **Stained Glass** A Charles Sewter p8
[82] 10 " p4
[83] 5 **Burne-Jones in Oxford** Ann S Dean p16
[84] 10 **Stained Glass** A Charles Sewter p8
[85] 10 " p9
[86] 5 **Burne-Jones in Oxford** Ann S Dean p16
[87] 6 **English Heritage in Stained Glass** p47
[88] 4 **Pevsner Oxfordshire 2002** p119
[89] 4 " p119
[90] 3 **Oxford Cathedral** S A Warner p96
[91] 4 **Pevsner Oxfordshire 2002** p119
[92] 6 **English Heritage in Stained Glass** p47
[93] 9 **Burne-Jones** Christopher Wood p23
[94] 9 " p23
[95] 10 **Stained Glass** A Charles Sewter p3
[96] 10 "p4
[97] 3 **Oxford Cathedral** S A Warner p96
[98] 9 **Burne-Jones** Christopher Wood p23
[99] 10 **Stained Glass** A Charles Sewter p6
[100] 10 " p6
[101] 10 " p6
[102] 10 " p6
[103] 10 **Stained Glass** A Charles Sewter p9
[104] 10 " p11
[105] 10 " p12
[106] 10 " p12
[107] 10 " p7
[108] 10 " p10
[109] 10 " p18
[110] 9 **Burne-Jones** Christopher Wood p23
[111] 3 **Oxford Cathedral** S A Warner p96
[112] 8 **Edward Burne-Jones** P Fitzgerald p52
[113] 10 **Stained Glass** A Charles Sewter p18
[114] 9 **Burne-Jones** Christopher Wood p24

[115] 10 **Stained Glass** A Charles Sewter p18
[116] 10 " p15-16
[117] 9 **Burne-Jones** Christopher Wood p33
[118] 10 **Stained Glass** A Charles Sewter p19
[119] 10 " p22
[120] 10 " p23
[121] 10 " p22
[122] 10 " p22
[123] 10 "
[124] 10 " p10
[125] 10 " p2
[126] 10 " p9
[127] 6 **English Heritage in Stained Glass** p47
[128] 10 **Stained Glass** A Charles Sewter p15
[129] 6 **English Heritage in Stained Glass** p47
[130] 7 **Wikipedia Edward Burne-Jones** p1
[131] 11 **King's Guide to Cathedrals 1862** p27
[132] 10 **Stained Glass** A Charles Sewter p15
[133] 7 **Wikipedia Edward Burne-Jones** p8
[134] 8 **Edward Burne-Jones** P Fitzgerald p264
[135] 7 **Wikipedia Edward Burne-Jones** p9
[136] 7 "p9
[137] 7 " p9
[138] 8 **Edward Burne-Jones** P Fitzgerald Foreword to 2003 edition
[139] 10 **Stained Glass** A Charles Sewter p30
[140] 10 " p21
[141] 10 " p13
[142] 10 " p21
[143] 10 " p21
[144] 10 " p14
[145] 10 " p21
[146] 10 " p23
[147] 10 **Stained Glass** A Charles Sewter p55
[148] 10 " p14
[149] 10 " p14
[150] 10 " p28
[151] 10 " p15
[152] 10 " p25
[153] 10 " p55
[154] 10 " p20
[155] 1 **Christ Church archives**
[156] 10 **Stained Glass** A Charles Sewter p22
[157] 10 " p22
[158] 10 " p27
[159] 10 p24
[160] 10 " p18
[161] 10 " p18
[162] 10 " p18
[163] 10 " p22
[164] 10 " p22
[165] 10 " p22
[166] 10 " p22
[167] 12 **Internet search History links etc**
[168] 14 **https://en.wikipedia.org/wiki/Edith_Hacon**
[169] 12
[170] 12
[171] 13 www.scarletfinders.co.uk/139.html
[172] 12
[173] 12
[174] 9 **Burne-Jones** Christopher Wood p24
[175] 19 **Myles Birket Foster Wikipaedia**
[176] 18 **Birket Foster** Jan Reynolds p90
[177] 18 " p89
[178] 18 " p89-99
[179] 8 **Edward Burne-Jones** P Fitzgerald p66
[180] 8 " p67
[181] 8 " ch 6-7
[182] 8 " p84
[183] 8 " p90
[184] 8 " p91
[185] 8 " p88
[186] 8 " p89
[187] 8 " p90
[188] 8 " p44
[189] 8 " p98
[190] 8 " p104
[191] 15 **Archives of Cheltenham Ladies' College**
[192] 18 **Birket Foster** Jan Reynolds p104
[193] 15 **Archives of Cheltenham Ladies' College**
[194] 18 **Birket Foster** Jan Reynolds p107
[195] 15 **Archives of Cheltenham Ladies' College**
[196] 16 **Time Was** W Graham Robertson
[197] 16 " p282-284
[198] 18 **Birket Foster** Jan Reynolds p104
[199] 18 " p105
[200] 18 " p173
[201] 18 " p173
[202] 16 **Time Was** W Graham Robertson p293